FROM "PHENE" TO "JOSIE"

LOUISIANA BAYOU GIRL

****

MARGIE MOORE

Published 2009 by Tanner-Moore Publishing

ISBN: 978-0-578-02073-0

CONTENTS

Ms. Moore relates this story in a confiding, conversational, and folksy tone: a matter of fact *that's the way it was* manner. As she covers Cajun customs, superstitions, and lifestyle it draws the remark, "I want to see what happens next," from those who have read excerpts.

From "Phene" to "Josie" describes Josephine's journey...

from "Phene" in her youth...

to "Josie" in her golden years

This book is dedicated to Mrs. Louise Stevens, who loved Josephine and furnished the author with priceless information about her childhood years. Much help was given by many people, so this book is also dedicated to all of you who played a part in Josephine's life and mine also with all manner of valuable help. You know how important you were and are.

Acknowledgement and thanks to Yvonne and Joel Williams, who were always there to lend a hand and give encouragement and be a constant blessing. Thanks for recent help to David Earl Tanner whose kindness exceeds any expectation. Much gratitude is bestowed to Donald Lee Tanner and Mrs. Linda Tanner for helping me with this newfangled computer.

To my readers: Thank you for choosing this book. I ask God's blessing on all who read this story and may you find it rewarding in some way for the time you invest in it.

NOTE: Martha's methods of dealing with Josephine's Alzheimer's may not necessarily work for others. All people are different.

The names Josephine, Phene, Josie, and of prominent people are real, as well as names of places. Other names were changed. (**Phene rhymes with clean**.)

m.m.

FROM "PHENE" TO "JOSIE"

LOUISIANA BAYOU GIRL

****

MARGIE MOORE

PROLOGUE

Josephine closed the book she had been reading to her two daughters. It was time to start supper. Her husband, Richard, would be coming home soon. The hot summer days were long and he would be tired and hungry after working in the fields all day.

"Aw, Mom, read us the rest of the story," begged Helen, Josephine's first born daughter.

"We don't have time now. Daddy will be hungry when he gets home and it's almost dark. I just wish I had more time." This is something her daughters would hear her say often. "There just isn't enough time in a day."

She went to the old wood stove with little Martha on her hip and Helen dogging her heels. Helen was never very far from Josephine. She followed her everywhere. Josephine asked Helen to bring a few pieces of wood and sticks from the wood box so she could rekindle the fire in the stove.

The old house was drafty with cracks between the boards of the walls, and it had neither electricity nor plumbing of any kind. Tonight it was hot; mosquitoes buzzed, and other flying insects circled when Josephine lit the coal oil lamp. As Josephine's brothers and sisters always said, "Phene has a hard life." They always called her Phene for short. (Phene rhymes with clean.) Josephine and Richard had moved far from their families to work on a sugarcane plantation.

For supper tonight they were having smothered potatoes, biscuits with butter, and figs that Josephine had preserved. The butter was made by shaking cream skimmed off the milk in a jar with a lid. Of course, Josephine milked the cow also. As she finished the cooking, she said to the girls, "I wonder why it's taking your daddy so long to get home."

"Ring-a-ling-aling," the girls piped up as they dialed an imaginary phone. "Ring-a-ling-aling, Daddy, come home. It's supper time." This, for some amazing reason, always seemed to bring him home soon. They often watched for him then ran out to the far gate to open it for him, and rode home on the sled Richard had made. Charlie, the big white horse, pulled the sled containing the farm tools while Richard walked alongside with the reins in his hands. Only after Richard had unhitched Charlie and watered and fed him would he come inside. He really loved and appreciated Josephine. Often he went to her to kiss her or just to pat her on the backside affectionately. Josephine never seemed to mind no matter how busy she was.

Richard washed up in the white porcelain basin in the kitchen. It sat on a small homemade stand with a shelf on the bottom. He shaved at the basin stand in the morning, looking at his face in the small, square, metal-backed mirror hanging above it. Daily bathing was done with a washcloth dipped in the basin. Baths in a washtub were reserved for Saturday.

Josephine had already carried in the water bucket she refilled from the cistern outside the back door. Rain supplied all of their water, which often contained mosquito larva. To collect the water after a good rain had washed out the gutters, they connected a piece of gutter to the cistern so the rain would go from the roof into the cistern.

The family sat down to eat together, enjoying the food. Josephine was a great cook. As Martha got older, she marveled that everything was good; nothing burned or spilled. Martha was clumsy and forgetful; she tried to do things well, but often caused a mess. Helen was the responsible one, and chided Martha about her mistakes.

When the supper dishes were done, Josephine joined Richard in the living room which doubled as the couple's bedroom. Richard was rocking both girls on his lap. Josephine took Martha from him and plunked down in her own rocker. Helen always got first dibs on Daddy's attention. Their entertainment was a battery operated radio which played The Inner Sanctum, Amos and Andy, and The Grand Ole Opry from Nashville belting out hillbilly music, as they called it then.

Bedtime came early since Richard and Josephine got up before dawn. From their bed in the adjoining room, the girls heard their mom and dad say, "Thank you, dear good God, for this good bed," as they sank their weary bodies into the feather bed. They said this every night, even after kneeling beside the bed to pray. As she drifted off to sleep, Josephine's thoughts went back to the childhood she left behind when she married Richard at sixteen years of age.

1

Phene's Childhood Years

Garry, Josephine's youngest brother, was full of energy and constantly picking on the others. "Jill, Phene hit me." WHAM! Jill's heavy hand slammed into Josephine before she could defend herself. Many times Josephine was the brunt of this cruel joke. She was innocent, but defenseless against this brother who was always devising a prank. When a rare occasion of candy or a treat came about, such as their dad bringing a bag of candy from town, the kids pushed in with their hand out to get one lest there weren't enough to go around. Garry got one, then held that hand behind his back and put out the other hand claiming he had not gotten any.

Once, Garry threw a rock and hit Josephine in the temple. Whether or not he meant to hit her, only he knew. Josephine talked about the things Garry and Jill had done to her all her life. She thought that Jill favored Garry. At least, the evidence bore this out.

Jill was the older half-sister of Josephine and her two brothers and two sisters, and ruled over the younger kids. Jill had an older sister, named Loretta, who had married and moved away. Their mother, Belle, died not long after Jill was born. Jill missed her sister very much, but she quickly adjusted to life with this bunch of new kids produced by their father's second marriage.

After Belle's death, with a short mourning period, Broussard, their father, married Jewel, a fair-skinned, delicate girl with black hair and a quiet manner. A young man with two daughters needed a wife to care for the house and children. Jewel soon bore him Broussard, Jr., called T-Brou, meaning little Broussard (Petite Brou) in the Cajun manner. Jewel then had Josephine and soon after Garry. Four years later Lois was born, then Carol. The family struggled financially although they all worked hard to make ends meet.

Broussard's father inherited a prosperous cane plantation, but lost everything to gambling. Word was, it was a card game of Bourre, a very addictive vice, which altered the family fortune forever. Josephine never dwelt on this which her grandfather had done, and her daughter, Martha, was thirty years old before she ever heard the story. Martha wondered how different her mother's life would have been if gambling had not factored in. Some of the others in the family were also taken in by gambling.

As a child, Josephine lived in a tiny wood frame house elevated four feet off the ground by cypress pillars. The house sat in a wooded area near Bayou Lafourche with a dirt road in between. There was a family of black people who lived nearby. They were of exactly the same financial standing as Josephine's family--quite poor--and the two families helped each other and shared whatever they could.

Josephine loved all her family and especially her mother, Jewel, who was frail and did not venture outside much. Jewel was a loving mother who fit the description of the Bible's woman in Proverbs as it referred to feeding the hungry. She cooked and cared for her family, and fed the numerous Gypsies and hobos who were vagabonds because of the Depression. Many of the homeless traveled on freight trains to try their luck in new places. However, the Depression reached across the nation, so work was scarce.

Broussard grew muskmelons and watermelons, and sold what he could to make ends meet. Josephine remembered him feeding the kids watermelon to curb their appetite and fill them up before dinner. There wasn't much money and sometimes the food Jewel cooked wasn't enough to go around, so someone had to go cook a big pot of potatoes. Beans and peas of all kinds, both green and dried, were grown, picked, and/or shelled to be sold or bartered.

Josephine and Lois were very close. They were the outdoor types, and loved to roam the fields and woods. Once the weather warmed a bit by late March, Josephine and Lois got their crawfishing gear together and headed for the shallow canals and ditches filled with spring rains. A few straight sticks or cane reeds with string tied on the end served as their poles. Any kind of bait such as chicken guts, salt pork, or fish heads tied on the end of the string sent out an attractive stink to the crawfish. The water was muddied a bit so the crawfish would not see them and shy away.

Then they swung the baited line out and dropped it into the water. It took patience to wait for the aroma of the bait to drift out and entice the crawfish into grabbing and eating the bait.

With one hand carefully lifting the pole to get the bait off the bottom, the other hand--sometimes the other person--gave the net a long sweep, and, with luck, didn't miss the bait with the crawfish holding on by their pincers. Sometimes the girls reached into the net to pick the crawfish from twigs or pond grass. Other times, when they had a net full of grass, they dumped the contents on the ground. Neither of them was afraid to grab the crawfish and put them in the old bucket they brought with them.

"Look, Phene, this one's a big one." Lois held the big red crawfish by the head section behind the snapping claws. The crawfish thrashed his tail attempting to swim away even as it was held in the air. To swim, crawfish spread out the little fins on the sides of the tip of their tails and pull their tails toward the underside of their bodies. This propels them backwards with darting speed. This particular one, however, was doomed to become dinner.

"Yeah, Lois, we got a lot of nice ones." They threw tiny crawfish back into the water to grow some more.

"Mom will be glad we got so many good ones. It's gittin' late and we better git on home"

"Phene, can we come back tomorrow and catch some more?"

"Sure, Lois, there's still plenty left. We didn't near 'bout catch 'em all."

The girls gathered everything and began walking home. "Phene, you know Sadie..., she told me when she caught some crawfish she put water in the bucket to keep them alive. She never knew they'd drown. It's funny how they live under the water but still need to breathe."

"Yeah, that's why we put them in a dry bucket. We *know* better."

The girls sometimes caught fresh water crabs in Bayou Lafourche with the same pole and net method.

By the time the girls got home, Garry and T-Brou had been sent to bring the cows in to milk. Jill was recruited to boil water and help prepare the crawfish while the boys took their turns milking the cows.

"Y'all caught some nice crawfish. Supper will be good tonight," remarked Jewel.

"Garry, you milk Sassy and I'll milk Pansy," coaxed T-Brou.

"Unh-unh, I milked Sassy last time, and besides, she won't stay still. You know sometimes she kicks the bucket and I don't want a whippin' for spillin' the milk." So T-Brou milked Sassy. They put ropes around the cow's necks tied to the fence post to keep them from moving away, but the cows were still free to move their bodies. When they finished milking the cows, the boys had collected a total of a pail and a half of milk. Next they untied the cows and let their calves out of the small pen that held them during the milking. Now the calves could run to their mothers for their supper. There was still plenty of milk left for them, and there was no shortage of fresh grass for the cows to eat. Sometimes they got a little corn, and chewed on the cob for any morsel that was left.

Everyone had chores, and the younger girls were sent to gather wood and sticks for the wood stove. Sometimes dried corn cobs were also used as firewood. While Jill stoked the fire in the stove, Josephine put the crawfish into a pan of cold water with salt to purge them then poured the water off. As the large pot of water came to a boil, Josephine put the crawfish into it, scalding them, making them a bright red color, and then ladled them out. When the crawfish cooled enough to handle, the girls broke off the tails and peeled them one by one, shaking the abdominal fat from the heads into the dish of tails. Next, the crawfish tails were sautéed in an old iron skillet with a small dollop of lard.

Meanwhile, Jewel took some of the fresh eggs that had been gathered from the hen house, broke them into a bowl, and scrambled them with a fork. She added salt, pepper, and fresh chopped shallots from the garden, then poured them into the skillet with the crawfish. As the eggs cooked, they were stirred around until done. The aroma of the wonderful crawfish and egg dinner drew the family in. The green onions really made the dish smell delicious. They had French fries made with potatoes sliced extra large and sprinkled with salt and black pepper before frying them, and also homemade bread.

Everyone sat down, made the Sign of the Cross, saying either aloud or silently, "In the name of the Father, the Son, and the Holy Ghost," as they touched their forehead, breastbone, left shoulder and right shoulder in that order. The Sign of the Cross was a Catholic tradition before and after prayer, and for other occasions. So they gave God thanks for the food.

This was a delicious feast, and there was much smacking of lips as they ate. Lois could see their appreciation and said, "Phene and me, we're goin' to go and catch some more tomorrow." There was a lot of agreement that it was a great idea, and everyone said, "Yeah, y'all do that!"

The house was shotgun style--only the width of one room--with the rooms one behind the other. Only a narrow hall connected the first and last rooms. The first room off the little porch was the living room, doubling as the parent's bedroom. The three girls had the middle room for their bedroom and the two boys slept in cots in the last room, the kitchen.

Laundry was done in the yard in good weather; otherwise it was done in the kitchen so the wood stove could provide hot water and warm the room. Dirty clothes first soaked in a large washtub filled by hand with buckets of water from the barrels which caught rainwater outside. (Drinking water came from a well.) A washboard, the top part leaning against the inside of the tub, and the "feet" resting on the bottom, held a bar of light brown commercially made soap on the little ledge above the ribs. The washboard was of wood except for the corrugated metal ribs. The soap cleaned deeply. It had many uses such as household cleaner and even catfish bait.

An item of clothing was pulled up on the ribs of the washboard and the soap was rubbed on it, then the bar was replaced on the ledge. Jewel, or one of the girls who were washing the clothes, then flipped the garment soap side down against the ribs and rubbed it up and down, causing the soap to lather on the cloth. As they dipped it down into the water and back on the ribs, they repeated the process to loosen any dirt. When the garment was clean, they twisted it to remove the excess water, and threw it into the rinse tub. There they swished it around to get the soap out and wrung it again before throwing it into a bucket or dishpan to bring outside to the clothesline where they hung them to dry. The clothesline was usually of wire about 1/8 inch thick with each end fastened to the tops of two tall posts in the ground. A long, thin pole with a V shaped end held the wire high in the middle as the clothes weighed it down. The V of the pole was placed under the wire and the other end braced on the ground, so it was adjustable.

Most people did the washing on Monday and ironing on Tuesday. They usually put a pot of red beans and some rice to cook while doing laundry because it cooked on it's own as long as it had enough water and was stirred occasionally. Of course, the fire had to be kept burning. The tradition of doing laundry on Monday is probably why many Louisianans still have red beans and rice on Monday, both at home and in restaurants.

Jill and Carol loved to stay indoors. Neither had much energy or enthusiasm for roaming outdoors when they could stay comfortably inside. But there were unending chores so they were never idle for long. Jill was very fat even as a young girl; perhaps it was the inactivity or a medical condition. She became diabetic in adulthood. Carol was the pretty one and was teased for being boy crazy by her siblings.

All the children had dark hair. Josephine's hair was so very black it seemed purple. She was thin as a child and teenager, but had long, sturdy and shapely legs and a sweet smile that lasted throughout her lifetime.

Josephine had a deep moral conviction to always tell the truth, and if the truth hurt she tried to word it kindly if she was pressed for an answer. Her mother, Jewel, was probably the role model for this, but Jewel sometimes got angry and didn't bother mincing her words. This caused great pain, embarrassment and distress at school for Josephine when Mrs. Finch, her second grade teacher, decided there was an epidemic of lice in her class. She sent notes home with some of her students to the effect that the child had lice and the parent had to keep the child home and deal with it.

Jewel received such a note from the hand of Josephine. Being the good, clean, protective mother she was, Jewel got angry and wrote a scathing note to the teacher, stating that her children did not have lice. Mrs. Finch also grew enraged, her face turning red, as she read the note. She was quite cruel and whenever her charges displeased her, she made them kneel on large, dried corn kernels on their bare knees. All the girls, of course, wore dresses. It was sometime in the sixties or seventies before girls were allowed to wear trousers to school. This punishment was embarrassing and painful, causing some bruising and bleeding, and Josephine remembered it all her life, especially since she did not have lice.

Except for episodes like this, school was a pleasant experience for Josephine. She worked hard at her studies and had many friends, both boys and girls. She had a friendly personality, along with her sweet smile, and a kind word for all. She enjoyed outdoor schoolyard games, like hop scotch, hide and seek, jump rope, and even marbles when the boys allowed the girls to play with them, sharing their marbles.

There were not many well-to-do kids in that little bayou town of Labadieville, and the school had no lunch room to provide food, so everyone brought their own lunch, which was often potatoes. A real treat for Josephine was when she had a baked sweet potato. Another good lunch was peanut butter on thick sliced, brown, homemade bread. Paper bags were rare, and any paper was saved for re-use, especially bread wrappers, which were of brown paper. Sandwiches were wrapped in these papers. Their lunch pail was a literal small pail with the semicircle bail-type handle. It was used for the less solid, less dry food, like beans and rice, or spaghetti. The kids used their little lunch pails for these foods, provided that their family had any leftovers, a rare occurrence in Josephine's home.

At school, the lunches were all placed on the shelf in the cloak room until lunch time, when the teacher let the children file in one at a time to get their lunch and take it outside to eat. When it was raining, they ate at the table that served as their desks. In later years, one of Josephine's friends told her that often when she had brought a peanut butter and jelly sandwich for lunch, it was gone when she went into the cloak room for it. It seemed that she was always one of the last to be allowed to retrieve their lunch. She was always hungry anyway, but this was a real disappointment. She was always looking for solutions in life and when she told her mother about her peanut butter sandwiches disappearing, they came up with a plan. She was going to give the thief something to chew on.

The next day, she shaved the brown laundry soap bar into slivers and arranged it on the homemade bread, thus making a nice-looking *peanut butter sandwich*. She placed it on the shelf of the cloak room as usual and sure enough, at lunch time it was gone. She told Josephine she never learned who the culprit was, but never had her lunch stolen again.

All of the kids looked forward to school's end in the spring. Warmer weather brought more great adventures. The strawberries which were planted in the fall needed some work. Broussard and the boys gathered pine straw in the fall and stored it in the barn. Now the entire family was called out to place the pine straw under and around the plants, so as the plants produced flowers, then berries, they were protected from frost and rot. The work was not hard, but the bending and stooping was hard on the backs and knees. As the fruit ripened, the family all got together to pick the strawberries.

Soon after strawberry season, dewberries and blackberries ripened. These were made into wonderful pies, cobblers, jam and jellies. Sometimes the kids were able to sell some to townsfolk. Blackberries, smashed down in a bowl and sprinkled with sugar, made a delicious quick snack.

Vegetables were planted and needed tending, so the days were filled with activity. Swimming and fishing in the bayou provided great pastimes for the young children when they weren't doing chores.

Figs ripened in June and July. The fig leaves scratched bare arms as figs were picked, and only washing with baking soda water relieved the itch somewhat. Figs were delicious peeled and eaten raw, or preserved by cooking the figs in a vat with sugar and a little water until they were tender and sugary as the water cooked out. There was a great bounty of nature which made a good life even for the poorest of folk.

As summer gave way to fall, the air grew cooler. The sun sat lower in the sky, its rays slanting through the trees.

"Lois, Bitsy said she saw a few pecans on the ground yesterday. Let's go see if we can find some," suggested Josephine.

"Oh, yeah! I'll go get the bucket."

The girls headed out the back door to the cow pasture where the majority of trees were pecan trees. The first few trees they came to had lots of pecans on the limbs, but they were not ripe and the green hulls clung tightly around the pecan. It would be a couple more weeks before they would ripen enough to open and fall to the ground. Under the next tree they found some small, round, heavy pecans. These could use a little more drying out before they would be tasty. If they were eaten green, they had a bitter taste and feel that stuck to the teeth and lingered in the mouth, something like eating a persimmon that wasn't ripe. They would have to spread them out in the sun to dry. They looked diligently all around the tree trying to find every last one that had fallen before moving on to another tree. This small, heavy pecan would prove to be fat and full and delicious. Some of the larger varieties of pecans often were light and there was not too much substance to them. They ventured about a mile and found only four trees with a few pecans on the ground. But they were happy with the amount they found, and now they knew where they could return to look for more. The General Store in Labadieville bought pecans and paid two cents a pound. In any event, the family could make good use of pecans as another staple of their diet. With winter coming on, the pecans would be used to make candy, cookies, and cakes for the holidays.

As the girls headed back home, they circled around a different way, checking on other pecan trees. Near an open meadow, they found some Maypops. They were Passion Flowers, genus name *passiflora.* It is said that the beautiful flowers reminded the early Pilgrims of the passion or suffering of Christ. Why they were called Maypops, or that they were Passion Flowers, Josephine and Lois did not know. All they cared about was that they were delicious. They grew on a vine on the ground and ripened at the end of summer and early fall. The flowers were delicate and beautiful, flat with a center of purple surrounded by white petals and yellow fringe emanating from the center. The hard, green fruit grew until they were about the size and shape of a large hen's egg. As they matured, they got softer and wrinkled and turned from green to pale yellow, and then shrunk until they were nearly dried up. When they were ripe, the aroma was a pleasant honey-rich smell and taste which was mouth watering.

Lois saw the first one and dropped her bucket, yelling, "Maypops! I found some Maypops." She yanked one off the vine, tore the dried skin open and sucked the sweet, ripe, juicy seeds into her mouth. The girls found several and ate a few but took some home for the other children. When Jill and Carol saw them, they said maybe they would also go out looking for pecans and Maypops.

The family attended a Catholic Church, but it was about 5 miles away and hard to get the entire family there, so they did not go often.

"Bitsy is here; she wants to know can Phene go to church with her," Jill yelled from the door. On the outskirts of Labadieville life was not very exciting in those days, and Josephine loved going to church with Bitsy, who attended a tiny Baptist Church within walking distance.

"Bitsy, come in, it's cold outside," Jewel called out.

"Yessum, thank you," Bitsy replied as she wiped her feet and gingerly stepped inside.

"Sure, Bitsy, she can go with you," responded Jewel, "Phene, you ready yet? Bitsy is here."

"Mom, I wanna go, too," whined Carol.

"Me, too," chimed Lois.

"No, y'all girls are too little. Phene...?"

"Here I am. Mama, can you tie my hair?" Josephine emerged from the bedroom the girls shared.

A fire burned slowly in the living room fireplace. Bitsy, who had remained standing, edged over to warm her hands while Jewel tied Josephine's hair and inspected her carefully. "OK, Phene, you be good in church."

"I will, Mama. Bye." Josephine kissed her mother on the lips, a light peck as was the custom of most Cajuns, and ran to Bitsy, anxiously pulling her to the door. When Josephine and Bitsy stepped out on the porch, Lillie, Margaret, and Ike were waiting to walk with them to church. Ike was Bitsy's husband, and Lillie and Margaret were their children. It was a damp, gray morning with enough of a breeze to chill your bones. Thankfully, it was only a fifteen minute walk to church.

Josephine loved to go to Bitsy's church. It was loud and lively, full of singing and rejoicing. To Josephine, it was so unlike the Catholic Church her family had been born into, where it was solemn and no one ever spoke above a whisper, except for congregational recitals led by the clergy.

Bitsy was of the black race, (the black family who lived nearby). In fact, the whole congregation of the little church was black, but they lovingly accepted the thin white girl with the straight black hair.

In the early 1900's, there definitely were racial divisions, but that didn't bother Josephine or her family. People were people. The color of their skin or their economic level was of no matter. It was their behavior that depicted their character. Bitsy and her family were top-notch.

When they arrived at the church, some children ran out to meet them, and some of the elders on the porch greeted the group.

"Y'all jest in time. My, my, y'all sure look fine today. How y'all doin'?"

"Doin' good. Le's go in where it's warm."

The music started up as a signal to find their pews. Four women and a man stood near the organ in choir robes and began to lead the congregation in "Jesus, Hear My Prayer", then progressed to, "Oh, Lord, We Need You". Lord was pronounced Lawd. The music grew livelier and was accompanied by loud clapping, some dancing and a lot of rhythmic swaying. There was some hand raising and a lot of "Thank you, Jesus". After a half hour or more of singing, there were announcements, then a basket was passed around for the collection of tithes and offerings, of which the largest donation was nickels.

Then a thin teenage girl stood up to sing a solo in a deep throaty voice. The voice and melody moved the congregation to more hallelujahs and thank you, Lawds. Finally, the preacher began his sermon with readings from the Bible. His speech was slow, punctuated by "Hallelujah" and "How many know that...?" As he progressed, he spoke faster and louder and preached himself and the congregation happy. As he made a point or quoted a well-known scripture, the vocal ones in the congregation shouted *Amen* or *Hallelujah*. Josephine thought to herself how different this was from the Catholic Church, which was beautiful with high ceilings, stained glass windows, colorful statues, and the people behaved reverently, but was so quiet it was hard to stay awake. To raise your hand would have been to bring attention of everyone with a wondering and disapproving look. It just wasn't done in the Catholic Church. Here, however, was freedom and fun.

28

2

The Opposite Sex

Jill had soft brown hair with her hairline straight across and low on her forehead. That, coupled with her wide jaw, made her face square. She had dark brown eyes, full eyebrows, a good looking nose and beautiful lips. Nobody had ever called her pretty. And what can you do with limp hair in the south Louisiana humidity? She pondered her future because she was not as pretty as Loretta, her sister, or Carol, her half-sister. She was not as spunky as Josephine or Lois. And besides, she was *fat....*

"Jill, some people just drove up, and it looks like Loretta and Phillip." Jill jumped up to see if it really could be her sister. Since Loretta had gotten married and moved away, Jill felt the loss of her older sister like a hot poker in the heart. Her fat legs carried her heavy body at an amazing speed as she rushed to meet her sibling. They screamed and jumped up and down as they hugged and kissed each other. Finally they parted long enough for Jill to greet Phillip.

"It's so good to see you, Phillip. Why didn't y'all write and tell me y'all were coming?"

"Well, Jill, it just happened that my job played out in Belle Chasse, and my friend Dan said they needed some extra hands on the farm where he works, so here we are."

"Yeah, Jill, we just up and packed everything we had and drove right over. Do you think Mrs. Jewel and Dad have room for us to stay for awhile? Just 'til Phillip makes a payday and we can find a room to rent...."

Loretta was interrupted by a burst of noise. At the first sound of a car, all the kids rushed to see it. The occupants interested them less. Cars were a luxury they seldom saw. As Phillip and Loretta dug around in the car and found the bag of fruit they had brought, the kids' interest shifted quickly from the car to Phillip and Loretta and the fruit they handed out to them.

"Oh, I want a banana, no, maybe an apple," said Lois.

Garry took the apple that was handed to him and put it behind his back while T-Brou, Josephine, Jill and Carol got bananas. Then Garry put out his other hand for a banana, but Josephine ratted on him, "Look at Garry, he got an apple and now he wants a banana, too."

"Phene lied on me, I don't have any apple."

"Well, we have more fruit so the folks can have some, too, but for now it's one piece of fruit for each of you," spoke Loretta. She wasn't taken in by Garry's pranks like Jill was. She leaned toward Jill and whispered in her ear, "I got something special for you." Then they all walked up to the porch where Jewel stood waiting.

"Come on in, it's good to see you. How long y'all staying? Bring your things in. Loretta, you'll have to bunk with the girls, and Phillip, we'll make a cot for you in the kitchen with the boys. Dinner is almost ready, so put your things away and wash up. Broussard will be in from the field soon."

As Loretta and Jill walked into the girls' room, Loretta pulled out a pretty blue bottle and gave it to Jill. "This is the gift I whispered I had for you. It's a new perfume I got at Sherman's Five & Dime. I thought you could use something special just for you."

"Oh, Loretta, thank you so much," exclaimed Jill as she dabbed perfume generously behind her ears. "It's so nice of you to think of me!"

"You're my very own little sister, and since Mom died, you're on my mind a lot. I love being married, but I'm so glad we'll be close for a while."

Dinner was really lunch eaten at noon, while the evening meal was called supper. After the meal, when the kitchen had been cleaned up, Loretta said, "Dad, Mrs. Jewel, we want to take Jill into town with us, while Phillip goes to talk to Dan about the job."

"Sure, that's fine."

"Mom, can I go, too?" piped up Josephine.

"Me, too," chorused the rest of the children.

"No, just Jill. There's chores for all of you here."

The trio drove off to Labadieville, excited about the prospect of a new job and being together. Phillip drove past the town for two miles and turned off on a dirt road which led to a small white house. As they exited the car, Dan came out to meet them. He was a good looking man, tall with thick black hair. Jill was glad she had put on her new perfume.

"Dan, please meet my wife, Loretta, and her sister, Jill. Loretta and Jill, this is my old friend Dan."

"Mighty pleased to meet you ladies. Mom has some coffee made. Come on in."

As the men discussed the job, the ladies made small talk, but Dan and Jill kept sneaking glances at each other. Phillip would be able to pick up Dan for work as long as he worked with him. The men went out to the car to talk and after a few minutes Dan said, "Phillip, let's all go into town for a soft drink at Bill's Drug Store."

Phillip returned, "Sure, I'd like to relax awhile before I go back to stay at the in-laws."

"Girls, come on, we're going into town for a soda pop."

Loretta said, "That's great. Come on, Jill. Mrs. Picou, you want to come with us?"

"Lands no, Child. You young'uns go have fun."

"Bye Mrs. Picou, thanks for the coffee," Jill said.

"You're welcome. Come back anytime."

Wow! Jill and Dan jammed up together in the rumble seat. Her heart beat fast. Dan was so nervous he could barely talk. Loretta and Phillip kept the conversation going for the two miles into town. It was Saturday afternoon and there were a lot of people shopping for groceries and other items. It was also a time to see people who were scattered in the countryside. Church on Sunday was the other social time, but unless there was a pot luck dinner, there wasn't much socializing done then.

Phillip stopped in front of the drug store and parked. The men helped the girls out of the car. It was quite a little chore for Jill to get out of the rumble seat, but Dan was happy to assist. As they walked into the drug store, Dan pointed to one of the two small tables and said, "Y'all have a seat," as he walked to the soda fountain counter.

"Hey, Bill, how about four bottles of soda pop?"

"Sure thing, Man," Bill smiled as he reached into the wash tub full of drinks in ice-cold water, where large chunks of ice floated. He took the bottles and opened them one by one on the opener that the soft drink company had furnished. The opener was a sturdy metal contraption nailed tightly to the wall. The bottle was placed cap first in the hole in the center and when the bottle was pushed down, the metal bottle cap popped off. As Dan pulled out a quarter to pay, Bill told him to put it back in his pocket; these were on the house.

"Thanks, man. I'll bring you some vegetables next time I'm in town." Dan walked to the table carrying the bottles and passed them around. He returned Jill's smile as she thanked him, their eyes meeting, and then shifting away nervously. The seat between Phillip and Jill was empty. Dan and Jill both felt a tingle as he slid into it.

Phillip and Loretta savored the icy beverages and thanked Dan, remarking how refreshing it was. The table fell silent for a moment as awkwardness set in. Phillip and Loretta could plainly see Dan and Jill sneaking looks at each other.

Dan took his eyes off Jill when he heard the jangle of the bell as the door opened. "Hey, Bae-Bae, what you doin' here? I never expected to see you 'til tomorrow at work."

"Hey, Dan. My mama needs some medicine. She got the flu real bad."

"Sorry to hear that. Hope she gets well soon. This here is my friend Phillip and his wife, Loretta, and sister-in-law, Jill. Phillip's gonna be working with us since they need some more farmhands. He's gonna pick me up as long as he works here, so you don't need to come by to get me. You can go straight to the field in the morning."

"Nice to meet y'all, we'll be glad you're working with us, Phillip. I'm sorry I have to hurry back, but Mama's waiting for the medicine. See you boys tomorrow at work," he threw over his shoulder as he headed to the drug counter.

Bae-Bae's real name was Richard. Since he was born, all his family and friends called him Bae-Bae, short for baby, because he was the baby of the family. He was good-natured about the nickname, except after he grew up and moved away where people didn't know his nickname, then a friend or family member visited and called him Bae-Bae in front of people. That was embarrassing to him. Richard walked with a slight limp. While plowing one day, the horse ran off with plow and all, tangling Richard in the reins and dragging him along. It injured his back and his right foot stuck out sideways ever since. When people saw it they called it a club foot. Even when he was still young, he sometimes staggered as he lost his balance on that foot.

The tonic that Richard bought for his mother really did the trick on colds and fever, but it sure was vile going down. There are no words to describe the smell or taste. It was a dark brown liquid which made you shudder to swallow it. A remnant of the Snake Oil of the Old West Medicine Man, but it never failed to conquer chills and fever. Richard clutched his purchase and walked over and said his goodbyes to the foursome at the table before he walked out the door.

All too soon for Dan and Jill, Phillip said they had to get back. Dan reluctantly said his goodbyes insisting that he would walk back home to keep Phillip from going out of the way to drive him there. But in his heart he was already planning how he could see Jill again.

Nobody got much sleep, but still the rooster's wake-up crow was not welcome as Phillip got up to go to work. All the adults got up, too, to start the day. Jill got the coffee pot ready while Jewel kindled a fire in the wood-burning stove, then peeled potatoes for breakfast and sliced the home baked bread. After breakfast, Broussard headed for his fields and Phillip to his car. Loretta walked out with him and gave him a luscious kiss and a big hug and said, "I'll be watching for you to get home."

"Bye, honey. See you tonight."

The drive to Dan's house in the predawn morning was interrupted only by a rabbit, which Phillip barely missed hitting as it ran back and forth across the road in fright. Dan was waiting on the porch and ran out to jump into the car as Phillip drove up. The field in which they would be working was just a few minutes away, and they rode in silence until Dan showed Phillip where to turn off the road, and then where to park near the tool shed. As they got out of the car, Richard drove up in his old, but shiny and clean black car.

Phillip would meet the owner later. The foreman got them started, then left for another field. Richard and Dan were old hands at farming and really didn't need any supervision. There were several black men who also worked there and they, too, knew what was required of them. They all spaced out three rows apart to hoe weeds from the newly sprouted corn. It was monotonous work for Phillip, but he needed the job and was glad Dan had gotten it for him.

Richard and Dan had worked together and had known each other ever since Richard had moved there with his mom and siblings. Dan's hearing had never been good and he could not hear well enough to know how to pronunciate his words correctly without slurring slightly. That didn't bother Richard, who had never even been to school, and besides, he knew how ridicule hurts. He was the brunt of whispers because of his own handicaps. So he and Dan had a mutual respect for each other and a close friendship.

At mid-morning, when they walked to the headland together to get some water, Dan said, "Bae-

Bae, you saw Jill yesterday, the stout girl. I think she might be sweet on me and I want to see her again. Would you drive me to her house Saturday afternoon when we get off work? I'll buy you some gas for your car."

"Okay, Dan, I'll do that for you. We can run by town after and I can pick up some groceries for my mama."

Dan thought about the prospect of seeing Jill again and his heart raced. Six more days to wait! Meanwhile, he tried to nonchalantly quiz Phillip about Jill, but Phillip refrained from elaborating about his sister-in-law. He did say he thought that Jill had seemed interested in Dan, and that to his knowledge, Jill had never had a beau. The days dragged by with excruciating slowness for Dan as he thought of the visit to Jill's house.

Friday morning, as Richard and Dan went to the shed for the shovels and hoes and other farm implements, Dan said, "Bae-Bae, I know we got to work tomorrow morning, but don't you forget now, I want you to take me to Jill's house. We can say we're going to see Phillip. Okay?"

"Yeah, Dan, I remember. We got to go home when we get off at noon and clean up first, and then I'll go by and pick you up."

Richard Robert, (pronounced Row-bear), was born to a pure-blood Cajun family in 1910. The depression hadn't hit yet, but things couldn't have been much leaner for the Roberts. Richard's father and mother had never been to school, and Mr. Robert moved his family around like vagabonds. He was always chasing a dream; hoping things would be better in the next town. When Richard came into the world early on a cold, damp February morning in Grosse Tete, Louisiana, two brothers and two sisters looked down on this frail boy with soft blond hair and blue-green eyes. Because of a genetic defect, the whites of his eyes were rather blue also, and he was destined to carry the gene of Osteogenesis Imperfectia, one of which characteristics was brittle bones. This disease was very prominent in the family, and few escaped it. Sometimes, there were even babies born with broken bones in extreme cases.

Richard had a narrow chin and a wide forehead with a little dip of hair in the center, giving him a heart-shaped face. None of the family knew much English, but fortunately many people in the area did speak French. Being Cajun-French, and illiterate, in a land of English speaking people, they were somewhat fearful of fitting in. Legal matters baffled them and they were leery of advice, unsure of whom to trust.

All of the Robert children were honest, hardworking, and uncomplaining. Richard had to work at an early age, because his father died just a few years after his birth, and as his older brothers married and moved out, the burden rested on him to make a living for his mother and sisters. Richard and his siblings did not attend school because of frequent moves, so he was handicapped in more than a physical way. But he had a quick, dry sense of humor, and a great deal of common sense and ingenuity. He worked at any odd job, and since agriculture was the predominant industry, he became a skilled farmer. He did begin to learn English little by little, but most of his communication was in French.

Richard and Dan had been buddies from their teenage years. They went to town together on Saturday and hung out with each other. By the age of 23, Richard bought a good used car. He knew how to do some mechanical work and he kept it clean and shiny. Dan supplied the gasoline since they were inseparable.

Phillip told Loretta that Dan had been asking a lot of questions about Jill, and Loretta teased Jill about

Dan. Jill loved it; the prospect of a beau! She did not know of the plans Dan had to visit, and had been nagging Loretta and Phillip about arranging another meeting. Her whole demeanor changed from listless to restless and back and forth from hopeful to hopeless. So on Saturday afternoon, as the dog barked excitedly at the approach of a strange automobile, Jill was the first one to go out on the porch to greet them and invite them in.

Josephine was lying on her mom's bed in the front room on her stomach, face down, crying and squalling. She wailed, "Mom, I'm hungry." She didn't hear the dog or the car. The smaller children were out playing along the bayou.

When Richard walked into the room with Jill and Dan, he couldn't take his eyes off the thin girl on the bed, with shapely legs exposed, her skirt riding high on her thighs. She was fifteen or sixteen years old and her raven hair spread out around her.

"Phene, get up and pull your dress down," ordered Jill. "We have company."

As Josephine rolled over, rubbing her eyes, she sat up and looked at Dan and Richard. Richard saw her dark brown eyes shining through tears from her pale ivory face, gazed at her rosy cheeks and red lips, and fell in love. He thought *this is the girl I want to marry.*

There were introductions, and Josephine quickly shut off the tears. She wasn't impressed with these men, clearly ten years her senior, but she was never one to cry in front of others, especially strangers. The manners her mother taught her to show to company took over and she was cordial to the men. Besides, it wasn't that often they had company, much less those with a car.

"Hello, Dan, hello, Richard. Please sit down. Y'all want some coffee?" All good southerners, especially Cajuns, offered their guests coffee immediately.

"Yes, that would be nice."

Of course, their entire dialog was in French. Josephine got up, straightened her dress, and went into the kitchen to heat the coffee. She told her mother of the visitors. Jewel went to the front room to say hello and check out the men, then went back to the kitchen to add more potatoes to the stew. They always grew a lot of potatoes, both sweet and Irish. The potatoes had to last all year and were kept in a bin under the house where they would stay dry and cool.

While Jewel added potatoes to the stew, Josephine put the coffee on the stove, took out the demitasse cups and saucers, and placed them on a tray with cream, sugar, and two spoons. She poured the hot coffee into the tiny cups, filling them less than half full, in the tradition of the Cajuns. When Richard and Dan put cream and sugar in their coffee, it was cold. The cream just sat on the top of the thick coffee until it was stirred in, because it was brewed so strong. That coffee could put hair on your chest!

As Richard slowly stirred his coffee, he kept stealing glances at Josephine. He thought of the irony of it all. Here he came to help Dan visit a love interest, and he had found the girl of his dreams! Sometimes a good deed has its own reward.

Dan and Jill were talking amicably, with more than a little enthusiasm. Richard asked about Phillip and was told that he and Loretta had gone into town to try to find a room to rent. Phillip had made a week's pay, and payday was Saturday noon at quitting time. The foreman had given them cash in envelopes with their names on them.

Dan and Jill kept the conversation going. Richard didn't speak much, but when he did, it was meaningful and with a dry wit. Josephine didn't have much to say either. She was still a little perturbed about being caught on the bed crying, and having Jill chastise her in front of the strangers.

The little children playing on the bayou started getting hungry and headed back home. When they saw Richard's car, they tried to outrace each other to get to it and look it over. As usual, Richard had cleaned it carefully and lovingly, and it was shiny and spotless. The boys jumped on the running boards to look inside. The girls also pressed their noses to the windows, awed by this shiny vehicle. There were not many cars around Labadieville and about the only time one came to their house was when the doctor drove over for a house call if someone was too ill to be taken into town. The kids had been taught to respect property, so they did not open the doors, although they all wanted to get in, sit down, and pretend they were driving somewhere.

Lois said, "I'm gonna go see who's here," as she ran for the house. They knew it was not Phillip's car. Before she could go three feet, the rest all started running and beat her up the steps, through the door and piled into the living room. They stopped short when they saw the two men.

Jill told the children their visitors' names. The kids didn't care who the men had come to see; they didn't have visitors that often, and no one was a stranger in

Jewel's home. All the kids chirped their hellos excitedly and sat on the floor. Lois sat near Richard, looked up at him and said, "Whose car is that outside?"

Richard told her, "That's my car. I bought it two years ago."

"It's so pretty. Can I go for a ride?"

"Sure, one day I'll take all of y'all for a ride. But not right now."

Jewel had got the stew going and came to sit and talk with the men, learning how it came to be that they would visit. The men told her they had come to see Phillip, but she was not a novice at romance. It didn't take long to see that there were sparks flying between Dan and Jill. It wouldn't take too many more visits for her, and Josephine, to learn that Richard had romance in mind, also.

Broussard had taken some potatoes into town to barter for sugar and coffee after he had come in from the fields. He returned with his horse, looking around for the boys. "Where's them lazy boys when you need 'em?"

He unsaddled the horse, brushed him, and gave him corn and hay. He also filled the horse trough with water. When he walked into the house, Jewel made introductions. Broussard greeted the men, and then excused himself to go wash up and change his clothes before returning to talk to the guests. He gave the sugar and coffee to T-Brou, telling him to take it to the kitchen.

Jewel called Josephine and Lois to set the table, leaving Jill, the little ones and Broussard to talk to Dan and Richard. When the food was on the table and the water glasses filled, she told them to call everyone to dinner. The dining table was a long wooden table with two benches running the length on each side. Four adults could be seated comfortably on each side. Broussard took his usual place at the table, and Dan and Richard were seated next, then T- Brou, while Jill, Josephine, Jewel, Lois, and Carol squeezed together on the other side. Garry was left to sit alone at the small table that was used for food preparation.

Jewel had cooked Irish potato stew in rich brown gravy served over white rice. She also had made a big pan of biscuits and brought out a jar of pear preserves they had canned last summer. The men were told "serve yourselves" first, then the bowl was passed down. They all silently prayed *Grace* and made the sign of the Cross. Everyone was hungry, so there wasn't much chatter, except for the little ones who always had something to say. Lois kept looking at Richard. She was drawn to his kind, quiet manner toward her and her family and she liked his friendly wit.

After the meal was finished, the men went out to the porch to smoke, with the little ones following, until Broussard told them to go into the yard and play. So they swarmed around Richard's car again. Meanwhile, the women cleaned up the kitchen and made fresh coffee for the men. Jill put out a great deal more effort than usual in the work so she could join the company sooner. Josephine and Jewel stayed inside until the coffee was ready, and again, Josephine served the coffee.

The afternoon went by quickly for Dan and Richard, and since Phillip and Loretta had not returned, they thanked their hosts for the meal and hospitality and said goodbye. Broussard and Jewel told them that it was nice meeting them and to come back anytime.

As Richard and Dan drove off, the little children ran behind the car following it far down the road, and then reluctantly walked back. Dan spoke excitedly to Richard, "Man, did you see the way Jill looked at me? I know she likes me. Her folks said we could go back anytime. I'll buy you a tank of gas every week if I need to so you will bring me back there, huh, Bae-Bae, please?"

"Sure thing, Dan, anytime. They're nice people. Did you see how pretty Phene is? She was real nice to us, don't you think?"

"Unh, well, I guess so. I didn't pay much attention to her. You sweet on her? You know she's real young."

"Well sure, she is young, but she's got a good head on her shoulders and she acts pretty grown up."

Dan was so pleased with the events of the day that he thought, "I don't mind a bit if Bae-Bae does like Phene, as long as he wants to drive me there." In those days, couples were heavily chaperoned, so maybe they would be allowed to court more freely as two couples rather than one.

The men visited the girls weekly. It helped that Phillip worked with them. It gave them a little more credibility to the family. Even though Phillip and Loretta had found a room to rent in town, they visited often.

As the weeks went by, it was clear that Richard had intentions toward Josephine, and Dan and Jill really hit it off. The foursome would often sit in Richard's car to get away from the noisy children. It was a good excuse for privacy, anyhow. Josephine was warming up to Richard, and there was a certain amount of pleasure in his attentions. No one had shown any interest in her before, and prospects were few in the area. Richard and

Dan often brought a bag of candy with them and everybody liked that! The kids all loved both Richard and Dan and always wanted to hang around.

Carol loved to tease them, and aggravate Jill and Josephine. One day she was playing around and by accident, got the tip of her finger cut off in the car door while the foursome were sitting in the car. She was a little less pesky after that.

Lois idolized Richard for several reasons. One of the most memorable events was shortly after he and Dan started visiting. It was Easter Eve and Josephine was boiling eggs to color them for the kids. When Richard saw her dip the boiled eggs into the dye, he said, "I wish I would have thought of it, but I could have brought y'all some sugar eggs." The family was so poor that Richard's thoughtfulness made a lasting impression on Lois. She was always tender hearted and loved everyone, looking for the good in people. Richard liked to tease Lois, and he often told her, "When Josephine dies I'll marry you."

3

Wedding Bells Bring Change

After working with Richard and Dan a few months, Phillip was offered a job as a roughneck on a drilling rig so he and Loretta moved to the Gulf coast. For Jill, having Dan to court her took some of the sting out of the loss of her sister as Loretta moved away again.

Josephine and Jill grew very close and the only time they went out was together because Richard had a car. The two couples went into town on Saturdays and sometimes there was a special event with music. Jill and Josephine loved to dance. Josephine especially loved to do the Charleston, which was popular in the twenties. Because Dan could not hear well and Richard stumbled a lot, the men were content to just sit and watch while their girls danced with other men. Neither of them minded because neither the girls nor the men with whom they danced acted out of the way. It was just dancing and fun, with no jealousy or provocation.

Early the following spring, soon after Richard's 26th birthday in February, he evaluated his position as head of household and spoke to his mother and the last remaining sister at home, Eileen. He told them he wanted to marry Josephine. They were aghast. Mrs. Agnes Robert didn't want to lose her baby, and she also didn't want to share his support with another woman. Richard's sister sided with their mother, but wasn't as vehement about it. Agnes also didn't want Richard to move out, and when she saw he was determined to marry Josephine, she agreed to the marriage and that Josephine would move in with them.

Richard had been seriously courting Josephine and she knew he loved her and wanted her. She had pondered the situation, and even considering his mother and sister, she knew she would have more with Richard and the in-laws than she had at home.

Her family, with the exception of Jill and Lois, were against the marriage. They made remarks about why would Phene marry that *tout casse'*, or all broken up man? They also wondered why she would marry such an old man; he was ten years older than she was. Lois knew in her heart why, even though she was only about ten years old.

Josephine's family knew Richard loved her and wanted to marry her. She already decided what she would do, and had told her parents. When Richard went to them they reluctantly gave their blessing.

So then on a pleasant February day, Richard took Josephine to town. He told her he had a surprise for her alone, so Dan was not with him, nor was Jill invited. Josephine kept asking, "Where are we going, and what is the surprise?" He would not yield to her questions, but stopped in front of Platt's Jewelry. Her eyes got big with wonder as he took her hand and said, "Phene, you know I love you. Will you marry me?"

She only hesitated a second or two and said yes. Richard kissed her and said, "Let's go in and pick out some rings", as he took her by the hand and led her into the store. Josephine gasped as she looked at the large array of beautiful rings. She knew that Richard did not have much money so she chose a set of thin gold rings with a small diamond.

St. Philomena Catholic Church

They married in springtime at the St. Philomena Catholic Church in Labadieville. Josephine wore a beautiful white dress she had made herself. Richard wore his only suit. All the family piled into the few cars they could find. Jill and Dan were their bridesmaid and best man and also served as witnesses. Everything went smoothly and beautifully. Sadly, no one had a camera to record the event.

After the wedding, they all went back home to find that the black family who had taken Josephine to church as a child had made them a wonderful wedding supper. Bitsy and her daughters, Lilly and Margaret, had cooked a big chicken stew with all the trimmings, and a big cake. They really loved Josephine and the family. So Josephine's wedding day was a celebration of love and joy. It was the beginning of Lois' sadness because her sister, her buddy and partner in adventure, would leave the house. That night began a new era in Josephine's life, also.

The wedding celebration lasted until the day was nearly spent, and darkness would soon fall. Richard was deliriously happy that this special day had finally come after he had waited so long. But now he could claim his beloved bride and take her away with him to love and cherish forever.

The family and friends all followed them out to the car, giving their best wishes and goodbyes with the admonishment that they should visit soon. Josephine hugged everyone, thanking them for their participation and help. When she got to Bitsy and her daughters, she hugged them all and said, "Thank y'all so much. You really surprised me and made my day special."

"Aw, honey, you know we love you and we were glad to do it. Be happy and come back and see us often."

Two weeks later, Jill and Dan also got married in the same church that Josephine and Richard had, but they didn't get a reception.

As soon as Richard had placed Josephine and her things in the car, he got in the driver's seat and leaned over and kissed her passionately before starting the car. That brought on the catcalls of oohs and aahs. But they were not embarrassed. They had waited impatiently for this day. By now, darkness settled in, and Richard drove as fast as the old dirt roads and the limited illumination of headlights would allow. It was about five miles to his house.

Josephine knew his mother and sister were not thrilled about the marriage, but she really did not know what she was in for. The women were not openly hostile, but they knew how to make cutting remarks. Josephine was not very used to that, except that her own family had talked disparagingly about Richard's age and handicaps. But she was not at all frightened to leave her family and go with this sweet loving man into her new life.

Agnes and Eileen attended the wedding, but were driven back home by Richard's brother, Reed, in the afternoon. So there was the faint glow of a kerosene lamp shining through the curtains in the windows and from the cracks in the walls when the couple arrived. Richard did not attempt to carry Josephine over the threshold. First of all, he was too unsteady on his feet, even though he was strong. Mainly he was a little embarrassed in front of his mother, knowing her disapproval, and they were carrying Josephine's bags and the few wedding gifts as they came in.

The women greeted Josephine and offered food, but she said, "No thanks." That was probably the only time she had ever said she was not hungry.

Richard left Josephine standing there and went back out for the remainder of the bags. He placed them down near Josephine, then took the kerosene lamp to his room to find his lamp which he lit, then carried the first lamp back out where the three women silently stood. Both Richard and Josephine were ready to get away from scrutiny at this time and excused themselves to go to Richard's room to settle in. There would not be much privacy in this house, except for a shut door.

Josephine looked around the room which was sparsely furnished. A fireplace on one wall was not lit. It was April and cool. There was a double bed; the mattress was stuffed with moss dried in the sun. Clean stiff sheets were under a coverlet that was made from scraps of cloth just like a quilt, but lighter in weight. It doubled as a light blanket and bedspread. A small nightstand and a chair stood in the corner, with a chiffarobe to hang clothes in another corner. Between these pieces of furniture was a chest of drawers. Richard kept his room very tidy. He was neat, but his mother and sister were fanatical in their quest for cleanliness, as Josephine would soon learn.

Being a country girl in a large family, Josephine knew a little about the birds and the bees. Her mother, Jewel, knew some old wives' remedies, and had access to some herbs and tinctures. Lots of people in those days were "treaters", to whom people brought the sick. The treaters prayed for them and did rituals to attempt to heal them. It was witchcraft, but they didn't know it and always finished the prayer by making three small crosses on the forehead of the patient with their right thumb. Ailments like warts, headaches, ringworm and others were taken to the treaters. They gave home remedies, too.

There had been scandals about loose women, some turning up pregnant out of wedlock, so Josephine was sure not to have sexual relations before marriage. She was only sixteen, but she had determination and was going to be married well over a year before she got pregnant. Perhaps her mother did share some of the old wives' remedies with her, because it was nearly two years later when she was eighteen and Richard twenty-eight that she gave birth to her first child, Helen.

Monday came all too soon, and Richard had to go to work, leaving his little bride with her in-laws. Josephine was used to a lively atmosphere with good natured teasing and lots of activity. The activity here was a lot of work without camaraderie. There was a small garden and a few chickens to care for. The women washed clothes by hand, and then hung them on a line in the sun.

Cornstarch boiled in a little water made a starch to stiffen the dress clothes. They poured it through a strainer to remove the lumps, and then cooled the starch before dipping the clothes into it, then wrung the garments out and hung them on the clothesline to dry. A heavy iron heated on the wood-burning stove was used to iron the starched clothes after they were sprinkled lightly with water to dampen them.

Agnes and Eileen were glad to share the chores with Josephine. Working for perfectionists who couldn't be pleased was difficult for Josephine, and she was lonely for her family. But she was well versed in keeping house, gardens, and animals. Agnes and Eileen grudgingly and silently admired her capability and willingness to work hard.

Richard loved her so much and was so kind to her that she grew to love and appreciate him more and more. He was a hard worker who didn't waste money, and from Josephine's point of view, feeding four people instead of eight or more was a lot easier so there was more food to go around. If Josephine wanted anything and he could provide it, he never denied her. However, she was a saver and didn't buy anything that was not necessary. When she did spend money, she bought the best for the price so it would last longer. Things made in America lasted better.

Richard was content in his spouse's company, but he was a social person who liked to go out. He was also proud to show off his young wife. They visited her family often, and occasionally some of them were able to visit her. Thankfully, the car provided them a chance to get away by themselves, and they still got together with Dan and Jill.

Josephine longed for a house of her own, but knew Richard needed to provide for his mother and sister, so she did not complain to him about the criticism she got from them. He knew how particular they were, and did have inklings that things were not very pleasant for Josephine.

Things continued this way for the first year. On their anniversary Richard brought Josephine some chocolates. A month later she conceived, and by July she was having extreme bouts of morning sickness. She was weak and queasy and one day she returned to bed after Richard had gone to work. She had already made their bed, and had eaten breakfast.

"Oh, no, get up and make that bed! You can't mess up the bed after making it and you can't laze around in bed all day," ordered Agnes.

"I can't. Don't you see I'm sick? I have morning sickness and I need to lie down."

"I had five children and I never stayed in bed and you can't either," Agnes said, grabbing Josephine's arm and pulling her off the bed.

Josephine had been raised to respect her elders, and she didn't want to make Richard choose between his family and her, so she made the bed. But no sooner was she finished before she bolted to the door and heaved her breakfast over the porch rail.

"Look at that! You wasted an egg," Agnes railed at her. "And you can't have another when you get hungry."

That did it! "You just wait. I've put up with your mean ways all this time but I've had enough. We are going to move out."

Fear gripped Agnes because Richard was their bread and butter. He was also her baby and she didn't want to lose him. "Grow up, Phene. Richard won't leave here. You can leave if you want to, but he won't go."

"Well, one way or another I *am* leaving. We never had much but my family is not stingy and mean like you." Agnes had underestimated the determination of this young girl who had put up with abuse long enough. Agnes decided to let it rest for now because she was not sure that Richard would be willing to stay if Josephine left.

Josephine knew how much Richard adored her, but she was not sure what would happen when she told him she wanted to leave. She spent most of the early part of the day on the porch with dry heaves when her stomach was emptied. Agnes told Eileen what had transpired and warned, "Just leave her alone today and don't say anything to her. Let's just split the work she usually does and let her stay in bed."

At last Richard came home from work. He sensed the tension in the air. His mother told him to wash up; she had supper ready. He looked at Josephine's pale, angry face and listless manner. Something was drastically wrong. He took her to their room and sat her on the bed. "What's wrong, sweetheart? You feeling bad?"

"Yeah, I've been having morning sickness and today was real bad. I came back to bed and your mother pulled me off and made me make the bed again. When I threw up my breakfast she fussed about me wasting the egg and said it was my fault and I could go hungry. She's always fussing at me and I am not taking it anymore. Eileen is almost as bad. We're moving. I am not going to stay here anymore."

"Oh, honey, I know it's been rough on you. They *are* too particular. I'll figure something out. Please give me a few days. I'll talk to them and tell them they better be nice."

"No, I want to go now."

"Okay, but let's go eat first."

Josephine was very hungry as usual, and being pregnant made it worse, so she agreed to let Richard lead her by the hand to the table. Richard was not the confrontational type, but he knew Josephine was dead serious. When she made up her mind, she could not be deterred.

Richard was silent during supper and so were the three women. They were all waiting to see what Richard would do. He had no idea.

After supper, Agnes and Eileen cleaned up the kitchen. They were not going to make waves, and figured the situation would diffuse. They didn't think that a little seventeen year old girl could make much trouble for them. She had always been docile. But in fact, Richard was working on a plan, but it would be another week and a half before a change would come.

Josephine had always had a good attitude and took things in stride, but after the continuing abuse of not being able to lie down, or eat again after throwing up, and critical remarks increasing, she began to feel resentment toward Richard as well as her in-laws. Her respect for Richard was weakening. She lost her cheerful spunkiness.

Richard knew he had to do something. He had been talking to his oldest brother, Reed, during their visits and they agreed that Richard and Josephine would move in with them. Reed and his wife Alice already had five children. But they lived in a large house on a sugarcane plantation about thirty miles away past

Donaldsonville. Reed didn't own the land but oversaw it. The owner was a generous man who appreciated having someone dependable to care for his place. So it was a win-win situation for all. But it was farther from Josephine's family and would isolate her more.

Richard and Reed spoke with their other brother and sister and the spouses. All agreed to pitch in monetarily to help Agnes and Eileen stay in their house and make ends meet. With that settled, Richard told Josephine what had been decided. Relief flooded her at the news. Of course, she would have liked a house of her own, but she knew that things would be easier with Reed and Alice and their five soft-spoken children. And so they moved. Josephine easily fell into the routine of the new household. Richard now worked with Reed since his old job was too far.

There were cows, horses, chickens, ducks, and pigs on Reed's farm. Feeding all those animals required buying large sacks of feed, in addition to the corn grown in the field. The feed sacks were of a good quality cotton cloth with lovely patterns and colors. When buying feed, the women got enough to make a garment and when the feed was used up, they washed the sacks and made clothes. Josephine was a skilled seamstress and made all her clothes.

The atmosphere was so much better for Josephine now than with her mother-in-law. She gladly pitched in with the chores. The women and children shelled the dried corn on the cobs in a machine. The husks were shucked off the ear before it was placed small end first into the corn sheller. As the handle was turned, the large teeth in the mechanism inside pulled the corn down and loosened the kernels from the cob. The corn kernels fell into sacks and were brought to a mill to be finely ground for cornmeal or grits, and coarsely ground for the poultry.

Reed was a friendly man with a generous nature. He had co-workers and other friends who gathered at his place on Saturday mornings to go rabbit hunting. A couple of his friends brought their rabbit dogs. They usually bagged several rabbits and most of them were given to Alice, after they had skinned and cleaned the animals. The women had been cooking while the men hunted, and now they fried up some rabbit to go with the meal. All the men were served the big dinner and dessert with coffee, and as they left, they thanked Alice and gave her a few dollars for the meal. Things were bountiful in that household and everyone enjoyed each other's company.

Josephine's baby girl, Helen, was born on a mild February morning in Reed's house. Josephine had women to tend to the birth, but the doctor was called out anyway. Helen weighed about eight pounds at birth. There had been ample wholesome food to nourish both mother and child. All the Roberts thought that Helen was a beautiful baby, which she was, with brown hair and hazel eyes. She had her dad's wide forehead and heart shaped face. She also inherited the disease Osteogenesis Imperfecta. Well, that wasn't surprising since most of the Robert family had it, including Reed and Alice's children. One of the girls had a milder case, but it was still there.

On Saturday afternoons, Richard drove Josephine and Helen four miles on the gravel road and three miles on paved road to shop in Donaldsonville. It was a nice outing for them. As they frequented the stores, the merchants came to know and respect the family, as did other people in town.

On Sundays they went to the Catholic Church, then to visit relatives, unless they had received word that someone would be visiting them.

Living with another family had drawbacks, but great benefits, since all the responsibility for the crops and animals were not laid on one family, so they had some free time on weekends.

Helen was the first baby of Josephine's family and they naturally thought she was a beautiful baby and spoiled her. To Lois, Helen was a treasure. When she grew old enough, Helen asked Lois, "Slee coco, Aunt Lois." That meant please fry an egg for me in Helen's French baby talk. It was the first thing she said when they visited Lois on Sundays. Lois loved to cook Helen's egg or give her whatever she wanted. Richard and Josephine visited her family and his every week.

Agnes and Eileen treated Josephine well ever since Richard and Josephine moved out of their house. They were content to live alone since they were cared for with the monetary donations and visited often by all the children. Helen was not the first grandchild they had but they still loved her. They didn't like the fact she had the disease of brittle bones, but appreciated that she resembled their side of the family and not Josephine's.

Richard always took very good care of his car, but it was getting old, so he put a down payment of one hundred dollars on a 1933 sedan and traded off his beloved old car. The new car was five years old when he bought it, but it would last him fifteen years until he bought another car. It was black and shiny just like the old car.

There was an opportunity for Richard to work on another cane plantation four miles from Reed's. Richard and Josephine were ready to have a place of their own, and even though Reed, Alice, and their children had been willing and generous to share their home with them, they were ready for their privacy also.

The other plantation was four miles farther from Donaldsonville. Mr. Turner, who owned the plantation, was a penny-pincher. Rumor was, he gambled and lost a lot.

The house Josephine would have was rent free, but no better than all the workers had, except, because it was the foreman's, it was a little larger and close to the plantation house. Mr. Turner's big house and surrounding buildings were grand in their day, but were beginning to show signs of disrepair. Houses for the farm hands, most of whom were black, were lined up closer to the fields in an area called the quarters.

Josephine was so happy to finally have a house that she could run as she wanted that the condition of the house did not deter her. It was a four room house, wood frame with board walls. Cracks were a half inch wide between boards in the walls. Exterior walls were overlapped boards run horizontally to prevent leakage from the heavy rains. A porch ran the width of the two front rooms with an exterior door to each room. A fireplace along the adjoining wall between the front rooms gave each room its own fireplace with a common chimney. These rooms were used as bedrooms, one for Richard and Josephine which led to the kitchen, and the other room was Helen's. By then she was big enough to be alone at night.

The final room was off the kitchen and was used for storage and as a laundry room with wash tubs. It also was the bathing room, and a chamber pot was the toilet at night. This room also had a staircase that led to the dark, spooky attic. Richard had to go into the attic whenever it rained to put buckets and pots to catch the rain that came through the holey roof. An outhouse away from the house was used to empty the chamber pot and for the daytime bathroom use. A quarter moon cutout served as the only ventilation except for the cracks between the board walls, so it was very odorous. Spiders set up their webs in the corners to catch unsuspecting insects. *Big* spiders.

There was a little room connected to the house that was accessed only from the yard outside the kitchen door. Richard used it as a tool shed. Outside the kitchen door on the opposite side of the steps was the cistern which held their drinking water.

The house had not been used in some time and was very dusty and dirty. Pack rats had carried in sticks and various other things. As they found something new to carry off, they left behind whatever they had been carrying. Josephine was no stranger to work and was so happy to have her own home that she just dove right into the cleaning. When Richard was not out in the fields, he helped clean the house also. Josephine's Cousin Gracie came to stay with them a couple of weeks to help get the house livable.

Their families donated a few articles of furniture, but they had to go into town to buy a bed and an icebox. There was no electricity, so the small icebox held blocks of ice purchased from a traveling vendor when he came by every few days in summer. The ice only lasted a few days.

The $17.95 chiffarobe they bought functioned as a small closet. It had four drawers, and a mirrored, lockable compartment above the drawers which held gloves, hats, and a purse. A large mirrored door on the right side of the drawers opened into a space to hang dresses and suits.

The stove was an old wood-burner with an oven and was already in the house. They also had to get a horse and a cow. A lot of work was involved to get this house livable. So, every night, when Richard and Josephine tumbled into bed, they said, "Thank you, dear good Lord, for this good bed."

Richard was afraid in the new location and put bars on the bedroom windows. During the quiet nights, ships passing in the Mississippi River blew their wailing horns, and that also was fearful to Richard. He never disclosed why he was disturbed by the sound.

A fourth class post office operated within the company store which was managed by the owner's son. Two fuel pumps--one for gasoline, the other kerosene--stood in front of the large porch which ran the length of the store. Nearly as much kerosene as gasoline was sold.

Down the gravel road to the left and adjoining Josephine and Richard's place, was a smaller store owned by Betty and Tom Robert, who had a young child named Gary. These Roberts were not related to Richard, and had cousins, two brothers and their sister, all unmarried, named James, Lee and Marie Robert. Everyone spoiled Gary because he was the only child in the family, but he was a sweet little boy with good manners in spite of the attention. These neighbors were very helpful and friendly. The whole community, black and white, liked the new family who quickly fit in.

Just as in Josephine's childhood, this place had a bounty to be harvested: pecans, pears, figs, and berries. There was a canning factory on the plantation which Mr. Turner also owned. He paid very low wages for picking the fruits and nuts. Anyone on the plantation could pick and sell them to his factory, or keep and use them. Dewberries and blackberries came in first, with the figs ripening in June and July. August brought pears and October began the pecan harvest. Josephine enjoyed gathering and preserving or selling whatever was available.

The area of land Josephine and Richard had for their use was three acres, plus five more as pasture for the livestock. There were several pecan trees on this land and two pear trees. One pear tree bore cooking pears and the other bore eating pears which were softer. They could also sell the pears, but canned most of them.

Richard spent his time building and repairing fences and pens when he wasn't in the fields. A corn house with a horse shed built on was a good distance past the outhouse. The feed trough was built on the back side of the corn house, and a large, cast iron kettle served as the water trough for the horse and cow. The barn, located near the house, held not only hay, but the car also. Richard bought a large swing and suspended it by two chains from the ceiling of the porch. It could hold three adults, or two adults and two children. The family enjoyed the cooling breeze the swing gave.

As soon as possible, they started a garden. Richard used the horse and plow to break the land. Both he and Josephine worked with a shovel and hoe to prepare the land for planting. They removed clumps of grass by shaking dirt from the roots and throwing the grass to the side. Using the hoe, they formed high rows. Richard made trenches for drainage with the shovel. They produced a good garden. Hard working people could be proud of their accomplishments, and there was no lack of good food here. The hard work made for healthy bodies and Josephine gained weight. She was not fat, but sturdy, and in her contentment, her beauty increased.

Helen followed Josephine everywhere she went. If it was picking eggs, feeding chickens, or milking the cows, Helen went along. Even when visiting neighbors, she sat in on all the conversation. Her weak bones kept her close to Josephine. Once Helen fell off the porch and broke her shoulder and arm. Any little mishap could cause her injury so she was not allowed to roam. That was just fine with her most of the time, because she loved staying close to her mother.

Josephine kept very busy but still found time to play with Helen. They exercised together on the floor, and played *Go Fish* with a deck of cards, did drawings and colorings, and Josephine read to her when she could. Taking care of the animals, milking the cow, gardening, picking and cleaning vegetables to cook, cooking on a wood stove, doing household chores, and a million other things all took time.

Josephine and Richard took Helen to town on Saturdays to get staples such as coffee, cocoa powder, flour, and sugar. In summer, by the time they bathed in the washtub and dressed, they were drenched with perspiration before they could even get into the car.

The roads were dirt and gravel, and it was slow going with washboard roads. The road machine, as it was called, came every couple of weeks to grade it smooth, but trucks and school buses soon made it rough again. Thirty miles an hour was nearly speeding, and with the car windows rolled down to stir up a breeze, Josephine always wore a scarf on her head called a kerchief. She did not like drafts blowing her hair or chilling her. Richard was hot natured where she was not. All her adult life she was known to always wear her kerchief. She seldom wore a dressy hat, except for a special occasion, or to church. Whenever she worked in the yard, however, she did wear a straw hat to keep the sun from burning her.

Sometimes the black farmhands caught small river shrimp. Josephine bought their shrimp and sold vegetables to them. When the ladies learned what a great seamstress she was, they asked her to sew for them, which she did. They brought Josephine a picture of a dress they wanted, the cloth and thread they picked out, and a dress Josephine could use to get the size right. So, from a picture, she was able to cut and sew the fabric into beautiful dresses. She made all of Helen's and her own clothes and often made shirts and pajamas for Richard.

4

Settling Down on the Farm

After moving to Turner's plantation, Richard no longer joined his brother in rabbit hunts. Richard had plenty to do with overseeing the plantation and getting his house, barn, fences, garden, and livestock in order. Josephine took on plenty of the work and organization, and helped Richard as much as she could. The workload was heavy for both of them. But the little family saw Reed and his family often. They allowed Helen to play with Reed's girls because they knew Helen since birth and had the same brittle bones that Helen had, so play was not vigorous. The girls played with rag dolls and had tea parties.

Helen was a quiet girl, and if she showed any athletic tendencies, they were quickly squashed for fear of broken bones. She followed Josephine by day, but she was really Daddy's girl. There was a special bond between father and daughter. At night, especially in winter when days were short, nights were long, and farm work diminished a little, the family sat in rocking chairs by the fireplace and listened to the radio. Helen always sat in Richard's lap. Josephine sometimes made hot chocolate and toast as they enjoyed a quiet, restful time together. She used a long cooking fork to hold the bread near the fire to toast the bread as the flames crackled in the fireplace. If she didn't have cocoa, she put granulated white sugar in a saucepan over the fire to turn it a caramel brown. Then she added hot milk to dissolve the sugar to make a mock cocoa.

In the summer there were afternoon showers every day to cool the air. Of course, it made for even more humidity than the usual 78%. Often, when Richard finished early in the field he would come home to repair fences, work in the garden, or whatever else needed doing. Occasionally, there was nothing pressing for him to do and he could get in a little afternoon nap.

Josephine got mosquito bars to put around the beds. It was a netting type material that let the air pass through, but kept flies and mosquitoes out. That was a great necessity on the farm, since there were no screen windows or doors and no electricity in the house. It was hot, and there were plenty of insects.

Josephine made a beautiful dress for Helen from a feed sack. The material was white cotton with colorful flowers. She made a round neck and puffy sleeves, and a gathered skirt with a sash. The sash was made of two strips of material folded lengthwise with the printed side together and sewn with a ½ inch seam on the cut side. She then turned them inside out to display the pretty printed side. Rather than heat up the iron, she pressed the seams down flat with her fingers, making little pleats to flatten the sashes and sewed one on each side of the waist. Helen always wanted Richard to tie her sash and she held her breath to make her waist tiny and said, "Tie it tight, Daddy." She never could get Josephine to tie it tight.

Whenever Helen wore a new dress and her cousins saw it, or Josephine mentioned making it, Alice immediately made or bought dresses for her own girls. She would never allow Josephine to give her child anything more than she could give her own children.

Josephine also tried to give her daughter new things which her cousins got, but too often she could not afford to do so.

At first, they had only a horse and cow, but Josephine wanted chickens, so she ordered some baby chicks from Lehman's in Donaldsonville, now eleven miles away. Lehman's, a warehouse type of store with many departments, had clothing, farm implements, hardware, feed, and seed.

Josephine asked for some White Leghorn and Rhode Island Red chickens. The chicks arrived in two weeks. They came in a cardboard box about six inches high, two feet square, with round holes about the size of a nickel all around the sides and top to give the chicks plenty of ventilation. Josephine kept the chicks in the box, placed in the store room adjoining the kitchen.

She got a container for water, from which the chicks could drink without spilling or turning it over. Raw oatmeal was their food until they grew big enough to eat finely cracked corn. Helen loved to hold the fluffy yellow chicks. Josephine let her play with them after admonishing her to be gentle. The extra bit of material on the tips of their upper beak that they used to chip their way out of the shell was still there. At night, when it got chilly, Josephine put a soft cloth in their box and they huddled together on the cloth in the corner of the box. Soon they grew big enough to be moved outside into the chicken pen Richard had fixed for them. It was elevated off the ground on wooden legs and enclosed with fine meshed wire.

Meanwhile, Richard was building a hen house made with boards. He put in a section of rails on which the chickens could perch. On one side he made some boxes with hay in them so they could lay eggs. This chicken house was large enough to walk into and gather eggs. Soon they got their own corn sheller and put it in the hen house. As Josephine let the chickens out of the chicken pen to forage, and fed them cracked corn, they grew used to their yard and hen house. Raising your own chickens guaranteed loyalty. They knew where home was and never strayed far.

As the chickens grew they had a natural instinct to perch, and they gladly left the pen to sleep in the hen house. Occasionally, an opossum would come around at night to steal a meal of poultry and the chickens went berserk, cackling and squawking loudly, so Richard hurried out with a headlight and his shotgun to kill the thieving 'possum. Richard decided it was time to get a dog to warn of trespassers, so he did and kept him on a long, light chain by the side of the house and not too far from the hen house. Of course, he had to build a doghouse now. The work went on.

Soon Josephine was pregnant again. She knew when her period was two weeks late. She debated whether to tell Richard her suspicions or wait to be sure. He was ecstatic when she got pregnant with Helen so she was sure he'd be happy now. She fixed a special dinner and prettied up Helen and herself. She waited until Richard had finished eating, then as she went to clear the plates; she told Richard she had some news.

"Honey, I think I'm pregnant."

Richards' reaction was joyful as he told Josephine he was happy and kissed her. Helen went over to her daddy to see what he was so happy about. She clung to his knees and Richard lifted her up and said, "Mama's going to have a baby. You'll have a little brother or sister." Richard wanted a boy so badly. He wasn't too disappointed when Helen arrived because he thought next time he'd get his boy.

Helen was glad Richard was happy, but she was too young to comprehend she would have to share her parents with a sibling.

In another month came the morning sickness. Josephine again started throwing up, being weak, and even going back to bed in the morning. She did not mind the morning sickness too much, because she was free to do as she needed to take care of herself, with no one to criticize her if she went back to bed. Josephine continued with all her chores, sometimes just a little behind schedule.

When the birth date came around, one of Josephine's cousins, Rosalie, came to stay with them to help with the chores, the birth, and the baby after it arrived. When the labor pangs began, Richard put Helen in the car, and on his way to town to get the doctor, he dropped her off with Alice and Reed. Josephine had been to the doctor for checkups, but in the country babies were still delivered at home. By the time the doctor and Richard arrived, the baby was about to be born. The doctor commended Rosalie for the preparations she had made. A short time later, a healthy nine pound girl appeared.

Richard hid any disappointment in having another girl. Helen was his special little girl and no one could replace her, but he had enough love to share with his new little daughter. Josephine called her Martha, because Garry, her brother, had a girlfriend named Martha, and Josephine liked the name. Martha was born on a cold morning in early February. Richard would never have his boy, because Josephine never got pregnant again. However, Martha became his little tomboy.

Helen always recalled her daddy taking her to her aunt's house in the middle of the night, and leaving her. She was made to sit in a high chair all day until her daddy picked her up after dark. What a strange, lonely, frightful day, and what relief when her daddy came for her. When she arrived home, she just silently stared at this baby sleeping in her mother's bed. Helen was just a few days shy of her third birthday.

By now, Josephine's brothers had grown up, quit school, and moved away to get paying jobs. Lois also had matured and got very attractive. It wasn't long before she had a suitor who proposed. He was a loud, vocal man, very friendly and outgoing. Andy's conversation tended to be matter of fact and dotted with mild profanities. He worked for the city in a nearby town, and was a good provider. The couple's generosity and friendliness brought many close friends. Lois was the link in her family who kept her siblings up to date on each other.

Carol was now the only child left at home, and Broussard made her quit school to work in the fields. She cut cane, broke corn and helped with other chores.

Being the youngest and pretty did not prevent the toil in her young life.

With the beginning of World War II, both Garry and T-Brou joined the army. They made fine soldiers and neither got wounded. Richard, being a farmer and crippled, was exempt from the draft and unaccepted by the Army. That was a good thing for Josephine, because if he had gone to war, Josephine would have had to live with relatives. She was content on the farm and had compassion for the animals and loved to garden. Sewing and cooking for her little family were chores of love. However, if she didn't have to do other housework, she would have been even happier. Sometimes when she was very tired, she would wonder what her life would be like and where she would be if Richard had not driven Dan to visit Jill when they were younger. Her thoughts of *what if* were prompted by her brothers and sisters continually saying, "Phene has a hard life."

The war brought rationing of sugar, coffee, and other goods. The government gave ration books with stamps enabling people to buy those rationed items in a way that was fair to all. The rich were not able to consume more than the poor. The news given to the public about the war was rationed out, also. Only things good for the morale of the nation were reported. There were campaigns designed to bring out patriotism and support of the war. Women now were taking jobs previously held by men, since so many men were fighting overseas and the need for production increased.

Richard and Josephine started taking the girls to a Saturday matinee at the movie theater in Donaldsonville every month or so. Westerns with Roy Rogers and Dale Evans, Gene Autry, Hopalong Cassidy and other cowboys were their favorites. Prior to the main feature, a cartoon and a serial about the war and how it was progressing were shown. Soldiers marching and fighting, planes bombing, tanks shooting, and ships on the oceans appeared on the big screen. The Japanese and Germans were the enemy. For years after, when Martha heard a plane, fear gripped her, and she would imagine that if the plane dropped a bomb, it would fall into the horse trough and the water would keep the bomb from exploding.

Martha played outside a lot, while Helen still remained indoors with her mother, unless she was working outside; then she had both girls following her. Helen loved learning how Josephine did things, like cooking, ironing, and sewing. Martha was always told to go out and play, especially when there was company. Because of Helen's brittle bones, she was still allowed to stay with the grownups.

The little boy next door, Gary, began to come over and play with Martha, and sometimes Helen would join them. They liked to play cowboys and Indians, and of course Gary was Roy Rogers, while Helen always wanted to be Dale Evans. Martha had to be a cowboy or Indian, except sometimes they magnanimously allowed her to be Ginger Rogers, even though Ginger was a dancer, a musical star, and never played in Westerns.

Josephine read to the girls, taught them games, exercised with them, and sometimes she demonstrated how she did the Charleston when she went to dances. She was quite good at it. Josephine loved to keep the radio on the country music station. Ernest Tubb was her favorite singer, a heart throb. Of course, she had never seen him; she just heard him on the radio.

Soon Helen became six years old and began school. Martha had Gary to play with, but she was still glad to see her sister return on the bus in the afternoon. Martha and the dog, named Jack, got along fine, and Martha saw that Jack could sense the bus coming a long time before it was in sight. Jack also knew the sound of the family car and jumped up and down excitedly as he barked for joy. He did the same when Martha started school and the bus brought her home in the evening. He also knew when the family was eating supper and repeatedly jumped up high attempting to see through the window. He knew he would be fed after supper. Jack loved Martha. Helen, however, teased the dog, singing, "Jack, Jack, Jack, Cucaroga Jack, Jack, Jack." Jack did not like that at all, and Helen had to stay outside the perimeter of Jack's long chain. The rooster also had it in for Helen, chasing her whenever she came out. Josephine and Martha had to protect her from the rooster.

Sometimes when Richard got through working in the fields early, he took the girls for a ride on the horse, one at a time. He placed Helen on the saddle, while he walked alongside, telling her to hold on tight and trying to control the pace of the horse. Charlie walked very slowly to the road and then Richard turned him around headed back to the house. Charlie picked up the pace toward home so much that he nearly galloped, and Richard had to slow him down. This scenario was repeated with Martha in the saddle. Richard had to hold her while controlling Charlie, who always hurried back to the house in hopes that at last he would get the saddle removed, get rubbed down and fed.

Once in a while, Helen agreed to play cards on the porch with Gary and Martha. They played *Old Maid* or *Go Fish*. One day Richard came in from the field and was taking a nap on a hot summer day with the door open. The kids were trying to keep quiet so as not to disturb Richard's nap, when a chicken in the yard walked by leisurely and squawked, "Cack... cack, cack."

"Gary, can't you keep your big mouth shut?" yelled Richard.

At that, the three kids did some cackling of their own, but very, very quietly as they couldn't contain their laughter.

The girls sometimes used a cardboard fan with a wooden handle to fan Richard as he napped on very hot days. He worked really hard, and they loved their dad. He was always good to them. Martha knew that Helen was his favorite, but she didn't mind, because she and Helen both knew that Martha was Mama's baby. Whenever anyone spoke of Martha to Josephine, she would say, "She's my baby." Martha knew how to use that baby of the family designation to her benefit.

Josephine did the washing, and when the girls were big enough, they hung the clothes on the line. Helen started on one end, Martha on the other. When they got all the clothes hung up, Helen started re-hanging every piece that Martha had hung. Helen was a perfectionist like her Grandma Agnes Robert, so Martha became the one that couldn't do anything right.

As Helen learned letters and numbers in school, she attempted to teach them to Martha. When she tried to get Martha to learn to spell her name and Martha could only remember the M-a-r, Martha cried with frustration because she could not get it. She was becoming a perfectionist herself.

It was really remarkable how well Helen learned in school, since she had been exposed to very little English prior to school, except for when Josephine read to them. Josephine and Richard spoke mostly French. Richard didn't know much English before they married. When they saw how important English was to the kids, they began to speak less French and more English when the girls were around. Josephine read to the girls often with one on each side of her looking at the pictures and words. They both gained a lifelong love of reading. Martha read practically anything in front of her. At meals, if the salt box was on the table, she read that.

The year after Helen started the first grade, Gary also went to school. His folks sent him to Catholic school. About this time, Josephine started helping Richard in the fields occasionally. Sometimes she had

Martha stay with Marie, James and Lee next door while she went to the fields. Lee drove the school bus for many years. After running two routes in the morning, he came home until it was time to pick up the children from school. Once, Marie and James took Martha with them to visit Matilda about two miles away.

Matilda was Gary's Godmother and had toys for him at her house. Now Gary was at school, and they let Martha ride his tricycle from room to room. The house consisted of four rooms, so Martha went around in a circle through the doorways in the center of the house. She loved it so much that they let her ride continually. Martha had never had or ridden a tricycle or bicycle before. But Martha really enjoyed the bike that day, so much so, that in bed that night she still felt like she was going around in circles. Or maybe the room *was* moving?

When Martha was still quite small, Helen followed Josephine out in the evening to milk the cow. Martha knew they would be gone a while, so as soon as they went outside, she went to the wood burning stove. She got some cool coals from it and started eating charcoal as fast as she could until they returned and caught her.

Once when Josephine had to bring Martha to the fields because she had no one to baby sit, she put

Martha on a blanket under the wagon while she worked with Richard. When she came back to check on her, Martha was not there. It took them quite a while to find her in the corn field eating dirt, because she didn't answer the calls. People said she must have been lacking a vital mineral to make her want to eat charcoal and dirt.

"Here, Martha, Mom gave us a meatball to taste and you can have the big half," Helen tempted Martha as she held out the meatball. A tinge of suspicion crossed Martha's mind, but it was only momentary as she took it and downed it. Too late! She recognized the horrible taste of asafetida, a brownish, bitter, foul smelling herb used in folk medicine. Josephine had begun giving it to Martha to treat stomach worms. She had to be tricked because she had become very resistant to taking the medicine. Eating dirt must have infected her. She tasted anything. Once, she tasted a root that anchored the corn stalk to the ground. It was bad!

Josephine seldom reprimanded or spanked Martha; she enlisted Helen to look after Martha a lot, and held Helen responsible if something happened to Martha. Martha loved her sister and looked up to her. But she didn't always listen to her. When Richard went to work in the field, he harnessed Charlie to the sled wherein he placed the shovels, hoes, and other tools.

On one occasion when the girls wanted to ride to the gate to open it for Richard, and then walk home, Helen got in the sled where the handles of the implements were, while Martha sat on the edge where the blades were. Helen said sharply, "Martha, don't sit there. Come here with me. You're going to fall on the tools and get hurt."

"You're just trying to be bossy," returned Martha.

"Giddyup, Charlie." Richard didn't notice the dialog between the girls or the place they were sitting. Charlie went *giddyup*, the sled lurched, and Martha fell on the hoe's sharp blade. The blade went deep into the side of her thigh, making a cut as long as the blade-- about five inches--down the side of her leg. As usual, Richard kept his tools clean, well oiled to prevent rust, and sharp. Josephine was bedridden with a horrible backache and her cousin Rosalie was attending to Josephine and the house. Richard had to unsaddle Charlie and drive the eleven miles to the doctor. Rosalie held Martha on her lap and applied a towel to the wound to try to stanch the bleeding as they went. The doctor had to put several stitches in her leg. This time Helen did not get blamed for Martha's injury. Martha was only three years old. From that day forth, Martha did whatever Helen told her to do. Well, almost everything.

One day, when the girls were still quite young and playing outside, Helen ran back to the house, calling, "Bebette, Ma-ma, bebette! *Bad* bebette!"

Josephine asked, "Where is the bad thing?" and followed Helen to the horse stable where she pointed at a poisonous snake. The large black water moccasin lay in the shade of the horse trough, then arched up and hissed with exposed fangs as they approached. Josephine got a large stick and killed it. Helen was a hero that day.

5

Making Memories

"**G**et up, Sweetheart; you don't want to be late and miss the bus," Josephine roused Helen. Helen was not a hard sleeper, and she readily arose and went to the kitchen. She stood on a chair and peered into her dad's little square mirror above the wash basin on the narrow wooden stand. She dipped her facecloth into the warm water her mother had poured from the teakettle, and soaped it with facial soap, then vigorously scrubbed her face at length just as she did every morning to go to school. Her mom said, "You're going to wear that face out."

For breakfast she liked coffeemilk with the end of the French bread. She was never a big eater. Josephine always packed a lunch for her, handing it to her as she went out the door. Every morning when Josephine kissed her and said goodbye, and sent her to the school bus, she admonished, "Be nice so they will like you."

As the school year progressed, Helen continued teaching Martha her letters and numbers. Helen was well behaved in school, and the teachers often delegated duties to her. Since she had the thankless responsibility over her sister at home, she enjoyed helping at school where the teachers acknowledged her abilities.

On Helen's birthday, Josephine arranged a treat for the class with the teacher, Mrs. Ross. Josephine and her girls made some cupcakes. The girls' major contribution was to lick the bowl, but Josephine let them think they were helping.

"Oh, Mommy, I'm so excited we're making these muffins so I can take them to class. I like to cook and share with other people," said Helen.

"Yeah, and everybody will know it's your birthday."

Helen brought the cupcakes on the bus with her. Josephine knew she would be careful with them, and would bring them directly to her teacher. Mrs. Ross said she would take the free time in the afternoon for a little party. Helen was immensely pleased not only to be the honoree, but also the hostess, as she distributed the cupcakes to each classmate. The kids really thought Helen was the teacher's pet now, especially when Helen began to help tidy up the classroom after the little party.

She made good grades, mostly *A*'s with a couple of *B*'s. The school had a program promoting academic achievement. It provided a free ticket from the movie theater in Donaldsonville to the student in each class with the best grades the first semester. Helen got the first ticket of the school year. Subsequent tickets each semester went to the student with the most improvement, so sometimes she won two tickets in a school year.

Helen was extremely excited to bring home the ticket. Her recollection in later years was that winning the ticket started the family going to the movies. The cost of a child's ticket was ten cents. Candy and popcorn were five cents for small and ten cents for large. This theater served salty and sweet popcorn and would put half salty and half sweet if asked. That made an interesting and delicious contrast. The honor of winning the ticket and presenting it at the movies was even better than taking it home, which was great, because her parents were so proud of her. "Wow! A free movie ticket! You made the best grades in your class. We are all going to the movies now," Josephine told her. "Your daddy will be so proud of you."

Martha thought her older sister was great all the time, even if Helen didn't want her to touch her things, so she was happy her sister was so smart. Helen always got something first because she was older. That's just the way it was. She was the boss because she knew how to ask, and *ask,* until Martha gave in. Besides she was fragile and Martha wanted to please her.

The girls watched for their daddy to get home from work as usual, but today he had three girls waiting, because Josephine wanted to tell him the news. "Daddy, Helen won a free ticket to the movies because she did better than the other kids in class," Josephine said. She and Richard called each other Daddy and Mama ever since the girls were born, and especially when they spoke in front of the girls.

"Good job, Helen. That's my girl. We gonna go to the movies Saturday and use your ticket," spoke up

Richard. Especially because he hadn't been able to go to school, he realized the importance of an education.

Richard loved to go out. He liked talking to people, enjoyed being in public with his family, and showing off his three girls. It didn't matter if strangers thought he was drunk when he staggered or if they mistook Josephine for his daughter.

Martha cried a lot, often for no good reason. When she did, Josephine teased her, "You're not crying right. Can't you cry a little harder?" Martha had a hard time crying when her mom said that, even when she was frustrated over learning her numbers and letters.

Josephine decided she should learn to drive and Richard was to be her teacher. That wasn't the best arrangement, but there was no other choice. Josephine was doing fine, even learning the synchronization between the clutch and gas pedal on the straight shift; however, backing up was another matter. She was attempting to back the car to park it in front of the porch and ran over the wooden steps. She broke two of them and Richard fussed at her for the first time ever. It didn't damage the car, but he got upset anyway, and had to repair the steps. This was about the only time the girls saw them fight. Josephine angrily got out of the car, swearing that she would never drive again. And true to her word no one could ever convince her to try.

Richard bought two pigs and a mule. He hired the mule out to Mr. Turner for one dollar a day. Josephine kept records of this and Richard's time, as well as the time of the men and women who worked in the fields he oversaw. Mr. Turner was not a racist: he paid the same wage to black and white alike.

Richard's time records

Richard was still overseeing Mr. Turner's crops and put in a great deal of physical labor. After a few years he rented a portion of land from Mr. Turner to farm for himself as well. His first duty was toward his boss' crops and whatever time and energy he had left were devoted to his own. Richard used the mule for his crops also, along with Charlie. This mule was more compliant than most mules that got the reputation of being stubborn, and he worked very patiently beside Charlie, pulling the wagon while Richard and Josephine broke corn and threw it in the wagon. Just a command from Richard and the animals pulled and stopped as needed.

Sometimes the girls rode in the wagon and pretended to drive the team. As their parents threw the ears of corn into the wagon, a stray ear often bounced off the wagon and hit them in the back. They did not mind. They enjoyed the morning glories growing up the cornstalks with their beautiful purplish-blue flowers, and the blackbirds and meadowlarks which sang them songs.

With only horses, mules, and hand plows, and so much hands-on labor, there wasn't much time for Richard's own crops. He planted cane to sell and corn for the animals. As well, he cut hay and hired a black farmhand named Clark to help bring it in and store it in the barn side of the garage. Richard called him "Clock." Since Richard didn't know how to read or spell, he often had misconceptions about words and mispronounced them. The girls always hung around outside and brought water or other refreshments to the men when they used pitchforks to move the hay from the wagon into the barn, and the girls call Clark "Clock", too.

When Richard fixed a fence and tore his arm on the barbed wire, he cursed, saying, "No good basket!" Martha was with him but never tried to correct his pronunciation of the word, even when she was older and learned the other word that sounded like basket and what it meant.

Josephine and Richard both had great perception and premonitions about events to come. After a couple of years of having the mule, they both had the same dream about the mule dying, and sure enough, that morning when Richard went to harness the mule, it was dead.

Richard and Josephine made a little money selling a pig or calf occasionally, garden vegetables, or from Josephine's sewing. Martha could understand her mother giving money to the people from whom she bought shrimp, but couldn't understand the concept of making change when Josephine sold something. She always asked her mom why she gave *them* money when she sold vegetables.

Their main income came at the end of the year when the cane was harvested and sold to the sugar mill. The price depended on the amount of sucrose, (sugar content) of the cane, which usually wasn't high until late in the year when it got colder. Richard had to see to the harvest of Mr. Turner's entire crop first, and this year there was a bad freeze before he could harvest his own, and his crop was ruined. The Federal Government had a program which paid farmers for the loss. This year's total income was only two hundred dollars given for the Benefit Payment.

A large department store mailed seasonal catalogs out and near Christmas, the holiday catalog arrived in the mail. What an exciting event for Josephine and the girls! There was so much to choose from: clothing, kitchen ware, tools, and TOYS. There were wagons, bicycles, trucks, games, teddy bears, dolls galore, and a gum machine bank with real gum balls. The girls were most interested in the dolls, even though Martha had a sweet tooth and gave a good bit of dreamy attention to the gum ball machine that would also bring money as it was used. Alas, she never got one.

"Sweetheart, I'm sorry there's no money for Christmas this year." Richard told Josephine.

"Don't worry, honey, the girls are young and won't notice. I'll bake and sew and they will still have presents. We know you worked hard and did your best. You had to save Mr. Turner's crop first, and we just had an early freeze before saving ours, that's all."

Josephine made cakes, clothes for the girls' Christmas presents, and bought candy and fruit for the stockings, but the only gifts they could afford for the girls that year were a yo-yo for Helen and a rattle ball for Martha.

The girls did wonder why Santa Claus and the Easter Bunny gave other kids so much more than they got, but Josephine was sure to do everything she could to make the Holidays fun. They cut a cedar tree from the pasture and placed it in the tree stand, making sure that it never ran out of water. She bought garlands and bulbs for the tree, and some very heavy tinsel icicles.

At the Five & Dime store she found some beautiful red and green paper bells about nine inches high. These had a string on top for hanging, and the bells folded down flat for storage. Josephine opened the bells by pulling the two cardboard tabs on the sides apart and brought them together on the backside until the beautiful bell appeared. A little clip held the tabs so the bells remained open. The inch wide strips of colored paper glued about two inches apart continually in a mesh pattern formed the bell when opened. The red and green bells hung alternately on a garland stretched across her bedroom, which of course also served as the living room. The tree fascinated the girls as they thought of Santa coming and also of the baby Jesus Christ for whom this holiday was named.

After the bulbs and garland were put on the tree, Josephine let the girls help with the final decoration, the tinsel. It was easy to put it on the branches because each strand was heavy and hung straight down, just like real icicles. It was also the first decoration to be removed for storage after Christmas. Each strand was carefully draped alongside the others around the cardboard before sliding it back into the box to keep the strands from tangling. This same box of tinsel served year after year. In subsequent years when only light, easily tangled tinsel was available, the girls lamented for the fabulous tinsel they had as a child. Josephine took good care of whatever she had and it was useful for many years.

The Catholic Church had Midnight Mass on Christmas Eve, and the little family made the eleven mile trip at night on the gravel road to attend. It was exciting to travel at night. There was usually a rabbit in the road, or some other nocturnal animal to see. Sometimes a rabbit did not get off the road and as the car passed over it, it jumped with fright into the undercarriage of the car and died. They could hear the thump as it hit. Richard stopped the car to get the rabbit which wasn't bruised and they took it home to skin it to cook. The girls were tired by the time they headed home and sometimes they would lie down on the back seat with their legs together in the middle and their heads near the window. Usually it was a clear, cold night with millions of stars twinkling above. As the girls looked up into the night sky, it seemed the stars were following them.

Christmas Eve was also Josephine's birthday, which was lost in the excitement of Christmas. But she never failed to get Christmas and birthday cards from her mother and brothers and sisters, and they often put money in the envelope. She would rather make a dress for her children than use the money for herself when money was tight. Richard was so content with his family that he never desired much for himself and always wanted more for his family. He rarely went anywhere without Josephine, but when there was an occasion to go to New Orleans with James next door, he always brought home a little gift for Josephine and some maple nut candies for the girls, who excitedly threw themselves at him when he returned. The girls were overwhelmed with joy when their Dad thought of them like this.

On Christmas Day, with great expectation, the girls jumped out of bed to see what was under the tree. There was always the fruit in the stockings: apples, oranges, and bananas. Gaily wrapped packages lay under the tree. Helen found several for herself and handed the same amount to Martha to unwrap. They each had a new dress, some socks, and underwear. Helen found her yo-yo, which she treasured. Martha opened her package to find the rattle ball.

Josephine gave neighbors some of her wonderful cake. Cakes lined the mantle piece in the girl's room, where they stayed cool. She made pecan cake with yellow layers. Finely ground pecans stirred into the homemade chocolate icing filled the thin layers and covered the top and sides. Coconuts were punctured in the two soft "eyes" with a hammer and nail to let the coconut milk pour out into a glass. The girls liked to drink it. After draining the liquid, the coconut was hit with a hammer to break it in pieces. A butter knife pried the coconut from the shell. The coconut usually separated easily, but sometimes the shell had to be broken into smaller pieces to get the coconut out.

In the next step, a sharp paring knife was used to trim off the dark brown skin, leaving only the white coconut which was then ground in the food grinder. This was a heavy metal gadget with a screw down clamp on the bottom. It was clamped onto a table edge or wooden chair seat to secure it. Gears in the center pulled the food down from its bowl shaped top as the handle on the side was turned. Blades were flat and round with cut-out holes for grinding or chopping and could be changed by disassembling the handle and gears. As the food was pulled through the spiral gears by turning the handle, it was pushed through the blades which ground it and out the side to be caught in a bowl.

Josephine made red, white, and green coconut candy using white sugar, coconut, milk and food coloring. This was cooked to candy stage, then spooned out on a buttered surface into little mounds to harden.

Cooked sugar, coconut, and milk made the juicy filling and frosting for the thin white layers of cake. It stayed moist for days. Delicious! She made fruit cakes, banana, and pineapple cakes, too. Friends and family loved to visit to get some of her cakes. They always brought her something, of whatever they had, like brown or white sugar from the refinery or something they had cooked. Her sister, Lois, and brother, Garry, started giving her a few dollars when they visited, saying, "Phene has a hard life."

The house was cold in spite of the baking and cooking. It seemed the wood stove with the fire burning in the oven would make it warm enough, but that wasn't the case. The girls pulled up chairs by the window so rays of sun rested on them, but the dampness of Louisiana made it seem colder.

On New Year's Day, Josephine cooked cabbage and black-eyed peas. Everybody in Louisiana had to cook cabbage and black-eyed peas to eat on that day. The cabbage was for money, and the black-eyed peas for health. Well, they pretty much had good health, but not too much money. Rice also was a staple in the diet of Louisianans. The complimentary proteins in the peas and in the rice combined when eaten together to make a complete protein for muscle building and optimum health.

As Josephine sold pecans, she saved up to buy wallpaper which she hung and pasted on the walls herself, then later bought linoleum rugs for the floors and painted the wood surrounding it. The wallpaper and linoleum were attractive, but insulated the house very little. The heavy paste wax she applied to the floors required vigorous buffing, so she made a game of it with Helen and Martha. All three of them sat on large rags and slid around on the floor until it was polished. When Josephine did exercises on the floor, the girls loved to imitate her.

At every meal, if there was no bread on the table, Richard looked around the kitchen until his eyes rested on the top of the refrigerator where the loaf was kept. When Josephine saw him look at it, she always got up and brought him the bread. All this was done without speaking.

6

Electricity

When Martha began school, Helen paved the way for her. She still was trained to take care of her little sister, which was a big job. Helen was there with Martha to catch the bus and showed her where everything was at school. All the teachers knew and liked Helen, and had a good impression of Martha from knowing Helen.

Helen had taught Martha first and second grade lessons, so Martha knew her alphabet and numbers and was bored in class. She sat in the back of the class talking to the new friend seated near her. Mrs. Ross made some futile attempts to halt the talking, and then gave up. This went on for six weeks, until her first report card. She made all *B*'s. Josephine said, "Next time you can get all *A*'s."

Martha purposely began showing Mrs. Ross she was paying attention, and in doing so, she spent less time talking. Next report card, she made all *A*'s and was awarded the free movie ticket. Martha worked hard studying and doing her homework daily, so she did well on tests. She was known all through school as the smartest girl in the class, but she had to drill to do it. Josephine helped her study, calling out the problems, and saved brown paper bread wrappers for practice writing. She conserved everything.

In spring, while the family was crawfishing together, Josephine spotted some tall plants growing in the shallow water. "Look, it's *herbe a' mal d' eau,*" she said as she walked into the water in her tall rubber boots and pulled a few of the plants by the roots. It sounded like she said it was *ab of my low.*

What's that, Mama?"

It's for a spring tonic. It's called *grass from the water for sickness.* I'll take the roots and boil them in a little water and make a tonic to drink. It's healthy for you. If you have spring fever or feel puny after winter, it'll make you feel better."

The family still did not have electricity by the time Helen reached her tenth birthday and Martha was seven. When pecans ripened and fell in late September, Mr. Turner, the landowner, paid four cents a pound for pecans. He resold them to pecan dealers for eight cents a pound, and the dealers in town resold them for even more. Josephine picked enough pecans at four cents a pound to have the house wired for electricity. Helen and Martha had been doing their homework by kerosene lamplight.

What marvelous change electricity brought! One of the first things Josephine and Richard bought when they could afford it was an electric refrigerator. They called it an icebox and for years after they still called it that, after the box which they filled with blocks of ice from the traveling vendor.

The night that the refrigerator arrived, the family stayed up until midnight while Josephine made some ice cream. It had to freeze, then be broken up, whipped and refrozen to make it soft enough to eat. Helen always remembered this with pleasure because her mother did this for them and made getting a refrigerator a memorable event.

Electricity brought a few more luxuries. Lights dangled from electrical wires from the ceilings. To turn the light on or off, a chain hanging from the bulb had to be pulled. The socket held not only a screw-in bulb, but an adapter was screwed in first, then the bulb. The adapter provided a plug-in for extension cords into which a radio or small appliance, like an iron, could be connected. Life and housework was getting easier.

Little by little, Josephine was able to afford new items. She bought good quality products that were made in America and they lasted many years. Now she could buy a washing machine, but she still washed the laundry in the storage room. A barrel outside the window caught rainwater. She had to go outside and dip a bucket of water to pour it into the washtub through the window. When the girls were big enough, they got water from the barrel and lifted it far enough for Josephine to grab it from inside and pour it into the tub. The rinse tub also had to be filled. Unless there was a drought, she took water from the main cistern to heat on the stove for laundry. The cistern was a little closer to the stove, but was outside and required navigating the steps. The hot water only had to be carried from the stove to the adjoining storage room and to the tub near the window. Once the tub was filled, the clothes were placed in the washtub and the process of washing with a washboard began, just as it did when she was a young girl with her family.

With an electric clothes washer, the agitator now did the work. When pulled, a lever on the outside of the machine's round tub made the agitator swish back and forth. After the required minutes to clean the clothes, Josephine pulled the lever back to stop the action of the agitator and took the clothes, one by one, to put them through the two rollers of the wringer which she could also turn on and off. The wringer could be swung out over the rinse tub, also. As the wringer squeezed the clothes, the water dropped back into the tub.

The girls begged to see who Mama would let catch the clothes that came through the wringer. Sometimes the clothes were bunched up going through the rollers, and the outside parts did not get wrung dry. They had to be repositioned and sent through the rollers again. Once in a while, as in the case of jeans, the rollers stopped because the item was too thick. Josephine whacked the red flange on top of the wringer with the heel of her hand to loosen the rollers, removed the item, re-tightened the rollers and sent the garment through again. The soapy water could be reused for another batch of clothes. If the rinse water was too soapy, it had to be dumped out of the window, and the tub refilled with fresh water.

The washer had a pump with a hose which could be positioned outside the window to empty the tub into the yard. As long as she lived there, about sixteen years, that is how she did the laundry. She never had a sink or running water in that house, and the basin and dishpan were also emptied outside through the kitchen window. The place the water landed, in the shade of the cistern, made an ideal location to dig earthworms for fishing. In her entire life, even when she moved because of necessity, she never had a clothes dryer, because the old houses either never had the wiring or the space for one.

Mr. Turner and his wife in the big plantation house had gotten a big black and white console television. Color TV was not invented yet. They let the girls go over and watch a program once when they first bought the TV. The girls found it fascinating and so beyond belief that they could actually see this in someone's home. As for the Roberts, they did without TV another eight years.

With winter, there was not as much hard work. The short days did not allow a lot of outside work, so the family had a little more leisure time. The chickens, cow, and sometimes ducks and pigs, plus the horse still needed to be cared for. Gardening was down to a few cold weather vegetables, and the sugarcane fields lay fallow and rested until spring when shaving the cane or replanting occurred. Shaving was done with a special blade-type plow pulled by the horse across the top and then each side of the rows in the spring, cutting down the sprouts evenly to stimulate thick new growth of the cane. If an area needed replanting, a furrow was dug down the center of the row from one end of the row to the other and cane stalks were laid in it and covered over with dirt.

Although they still received visits from family, more often, Josephine, Richard and girls visited down the bayou. With Reed and Alice being the only family close enough to visit often, the rest of their families could be visited a few at a time as they made their way toward them. So they tended to the animals, then got into the car and went. With all the family to see, they were always offered lots of food and did not have to pack a lunch.

Richard's mother, Agnes, and sister, Eileen, were nearest, with a cousin living nearby. Their cousin, Sandra, worked for a family who owned a restaurant and dance hall. Helen and Martha loved visiting Sandra. She was beautiful and glamorous. Besides, she took the girls upstairs to the empty, darkened dance hall where they could play. Sometimes they would find change on the floor that patrons dropped while buying drinks. Dance halls were always dark and nobody wanted to crawl around on the floor to find their loose change, so usually pennies, nickels, dimes, and an occasional quarter could be found.

At Grandma Agnes Robert's, the girls sat and visited awhile before going outside. Agnes or Eileen soon heated up the coffee and served it to the grownups. They did not heat their house very much; the demitasse cups were tiny and only half full, and with the addition of heavy cream, the strong coffee was even colder. With their move to the river, Josephine was treated much nicer by her in-laws and the conversation was pleasant.

The kids loved looking at their grandma's flowers. She had rose bushes and four o'clocks and various other plants. Four o'clocks opened their blossoms around 4 o'clock, and after an hour or so, they closed again. There were always a couple of pepper plants near the door. The little peppers were green, and as they ripened they turned yellow, then red. The peppers, placed in bottles of vinegar, made a delicious spike when sprinkled on a dish of beans and rice.

When they visited in the afternoon and the kids needed a snack, Agnes sat them down at the table in her spotless kitchen and sliced some of her famous homemade bread for them. The bread had a strong yeasty smell with large holes from the rising, and was smeared with home churned butter. She was generous with her grandchildren.

Then it was off to visit Jill and Dan. Since they had married shortly after Josephine and Richard, one would have thought that they would have had children, but they remained childless. Richard's other brother, Jack, and his wife, Olive, were Helen's Godparents at her Catholic Christening. Jill and Dan became Martha's Godparents. They were Godparents to one other girl, Lillie Mae. Jill and Dan were the perfect Godparents because they loved children and didn't have any of their own.

There wasn't much to entertain the girls at Jill's house, but there was usually lots of other company so things weren't boring. Richard's brother, Jack, and

Jack's wife, Olive, lived next door so some of the time was spent visiting there. Jill loved to cook meat balls, whether fried or in spaghetti. Martha and Helen were aghast, but respectfully silent, to see Jill eat chunks of the raw meatballs prior to cooking. What could make her do this? Even Martha, who faintly recalled when she herself ate charcoal and dirt, was grossed out by the idea of eating raw ground meat, even if it had been seasoned.

Dan liked to play with the girls, hold them in his lap and pinch their nose between his fingers, poke his thumb between the middle and forefinger, and say, "I pulled off your nose."

Helen was wise to this, but Martha always felt her nose and said, "No you didn't."

By this time the day was almost spent, and the family had to head back home. Many times, Richard stopped at a bakery on the way home and they got some shoe soles to eat in the car. They were a thin, fried, yeasty pastry with a sugar glaze, shaped like a large shoe sole; hence the name.

Martha loved sweets, having had lots since her birth. Helen loved salty, fattier foods like pork rinds and potato chips. Martha took after her mom, Helen after her dad. Whenever the family had snacked on lots of sweets, Richard said, "I want some salty food," meaning a real balanced meal with meat and vegetables, rice or potatoes. Since they had a garden, they did eat a nutritious diet, but many times, supper consisted of *beignets:* deep fried, slightly sweet dough, served with butter, preserved figs, and milk. Sometimes it was just cornbread, butter, and milk. They enjoyed it and didn't think they were deprived.

One winter night, Martha was helping Josephine peel pecans, and she dropped the pan of shells on the floor. "Martha, get the broom and sweep this near the fireplace."

"OK, Mom." Martha got the broom and swept the shells toward the door instead.

"No, don't sweep them outside. It's bad luck to sweep anything outside at night."

"Who said so?"

"I don't know. Just don't do it. Wait 'til morning to sweep it outside."

Another old wives' tale was to never sweep under a seated person, or that person would never marry again. Josephine never let anyone sweep under her chair.

More fables were if your nose itched, or if your right palm itched, someone wanted to kiss you. If your left palm itched it meant you were going to get some money.

Martha was careless and absentminded about everyday things. She often left her sweater or books in the classroom. Before the bus came in the afternoon, she and Helen had to find the teacher to unlock the door. The teacher grew aggravated at the frequency of this, and seemed to get angrier at Helen than at Martha. Helen tried to make excuses as to why Martha forgot things.

There was a day that Helen was sick and did not go to school. Martha joined a group of kids who were playing ledge ball in the morning, and left her lunch on a window sill. At noon, she began to wonder where her lunch was. She had brought French Toast in a brown bag. Josephine called it lost bread, or *Pain Perdue* in French. Martha knew Helen wasn't at school, and wasn't used to thinking for herself, so she found her cousin, Jackie, who was Reed's third eldest daughter, and was one year older than Helen.

"Jackie, Helen's not here and I lost my lost bread."

Puzzled, Jackie said, "What do you mean, you lost your lost bread?"

"Mom made me lost bread for lunch and I can't find it."

Jackie had never heard of lost bread before, but said, "Where were you the last time you saw it?"

"Oh, I was playing ledge ball. I think I can find my lost bread now. Thank you, Jackie." Ledge ball was played by throwing a small, solid rubber ball against a curved ledge on the window, making it rebound high in the air. Sure enough, Martha's lunch was still on the window sill.

Some people were making large balls from aluminum found on the wrapper of sticks of gum. The girls tried it, but never had that much gum to use. The wrapper was soaked in water to loosen the aluminum sheet from the paper backing, and after they were pulled apart, the aluminum was rolled and more sheets were added around until the ball could be the size of a baseball or larger if you had enough aluminum. Aluminum for wrapping was not available yet.

Martha sat on the school bus with Vickie, Jackie's younger sister. Vickie was a pale, frail girl that everyone wanted to care for. She had a delicate face, blue eyes and blond hair, as did Jackie. Martha and Vickie were always very close, even though Vickie was two years younger, but once at school, they stayed with their own classmates.

When Richard's family visited Reed's in their big house, Martha and Vickie played games like creating their own movies. Frequently, the older kids joined in. That was really fun. They would do glamorous movies, scary movies, and funny movies, too. Sheila was the best. She created scenarios that were hilarious and made the funniest faces. All the kids got along fine and never quarreled. Reed and Alice's kids were gentle and kind and Josephine still told Helen and Martha to be nice so everyone would like them.

One time, the older kids were off to the side while Martha and Vickie were playing a game where they had to run to a base; in this case a wooden chair. As Vickie ran to the base, she slipped on a piece of paper and fell, her nose hitting the edge of the seat. Everyone ran to her aid, putting an ice pack on it to stop the bleeding. She had a broken nose and a lifelong bump and scar, but that still did not affect her personality or attractiveness. Martha was always sorry that Vickie got hurt playing with her.

On the farm, Martha spent a great deal of time outdoors, and when Richard did chores near the house, Martha followed him, "helping" him. Sometimes she was able to fetch things for him, or hold something. She learned a lot about country life and fixing things. To fix the fence, she held the barbed wire tight against the post with the crowbar while Richard nailed it down with large staples. She was there when he took the shovel to dig drains around the house to keep rainwater from getting too near the house, or when he dug ditches to drain water from the garden.

Josephine kept books on Richard's hours and wages, as well as the hired help's time. In 1956, Richard worked sixty-eight hours between January second and twelfth and earned $43.16. *That came to sixty-three cents an hour.* Her little notebook held prior records in 1952 showing earnings of forty-three cents an hour. The black farmhands, male and female, made the exact same wage per hour as Richard. Being an overseer didn't help any.

7

Life and Death

In the summer, Gary Robert often came over from his aunt's and uncles' house next door to play with Martha. Gary loved Martha and would agree to any game she wanted to play, like hopscotch on the bare dirt, or marbles, knives, or doing somersaults on the sawhorse. Marbles was played in a circle with a line drawn across the middle. So were knives. In marbles, one took his "taw" and shot toward the opponent's marbles in the other half of the circle, and could keep any marbles that their taw hit and moved outside the circle. In knives, they took a pocket knife and threw it into the opponent's half of the circle hoping to make the blade stick up in the ground. Then they could draw a line dividing that half of the circle wherever the blade landed, and claim either half of the opponent's territory, erasing the line between it and their own until they owned the entire circle. Gary usually won, but Martha was a worthy opponent, and if she won at anything, it didn't ruffle Gary's feathers. He had confidence in himself and if a girl beat him, it didn't worry him a bit.

One day Martha wanted to make a mud cake. They called it mud pies. Josephine gave them an old, cracked plate, an old butter knife, and some rancid pecans which were not edible. Gary helped with the dirty work, getting some nice dirt and mixing just enough water into it to make it easy to mold.

Martha took over the job, piling the mud on the plate and forming it. She dipped the knife blade into water and smoothed it around the top and sides continually until it looked like a nice four layer cake and then placed the halves of pecans around the top of the cake.

That day, Richard had hired Clark to help him get some hay into the barn. Martha mischievously suggested they offer Clark some cake. Gary said okay. They carried the cake to the barn where the men worked. Martha said, "Clock," (just like her dad called him,) "do you want some Chocolate Pecan Cake?"

"Oh, I shore do!"

Then it was no longer a joke as Martha had to sorrowfully explain that they had played a trick and they were sorry they didn't really have any cake. Clark was even more disappointed than they were, "That shore looked like a real fine cake." Her dad was working toward the back of the barn and didn't notice; Martha was glad. However, they did go solicit some lemonade from Josephine to give Clark and Richard, to make up for the trick.

"Martha, when you and Gary go play behind the stable and corn house, do y'all ever kiss?" asked Josephine.

"Ugh! No, Mama, but he asked me to and I said no."

Summer days were hot; still there was always shade from the large pecan trees surrounding the house, and daily afternoon showers cooled the air but made it muggy also. There was never an end to the work for Josephine, while the girls played school until they tired of it, "Mom, I don't have anything to do."

"You could wash the dishes."

"Aw, Mom, not that."

Josephine had always let them do whatever they could, and when they were small they always wanted to help. Once they were able to do more, they weren't so eager to volunteer. Helen had been used to standing on a chair ever since she was able, stirring that incessant pot of beans. After a while the novelty wore off, but she still did it. Martha was never recruited to cook. She had too many clumsy accidents. Josephine did not force or coerce them to do anything more than hanging and folding clothes, cleaning their room or doing dishes occasionally. She wanted to let them enjoy their childhood: they would have enough work later when they were grown. Still, they pitched in with harvesting vegetables, digging potatoes, picking beans and peas and shelling them.

Josephine managed the household's money with Richard's advice. She was able to save money, no matter how little they had. She always said, "It's not how much you make, but how much you save."

Owls were heard frequently at night in the country. But when a screech owl screeched--they called it a switch owl--it sent a shiver down the spine. Legend said when a screech owl called, it signaled the death of someone within three days unless you turned your pocket inside out. Whenever anyone heard a screech owl, they looked for a pocket which could be turned inside out.

Josephine missed her family, especially her mother, and Jewel missed her, as did all her family. It seemed they never got to see each other enough. One of Jewel's letters to Josephine began, "My darling, how we miss you and pray you are doing well. We never get enough news from you and don't get to see you often." This letter was an outpouring of love and longing. Broussard and Jewel were seldom able to make the long trip to the farm, and had to depend on the small amount of time that Josephine and Richard could share with them when they went to visit all the relatives.

Josephine kept the letters and cards she got from her family as long as she lived. Many of them contained a few dollars to help out. Especially on her birthday, they sent money hoping she would get something for herself, and sometimes she would buy a nice piece of fabric, thread, buttons, lace and rick rack to make dresses. Most often money came from Lois or Jill, but even Garry sent birthday or Christmas cards with money. And they still said, "Phene has a hard life."

Jewel practiced fortune telling, using cards, and it was said that she foretold her own death with a deck of cards turning up a black queen.

Garry married Isabel after his stint in the Army. She was a small, dark haired girl who was meticulous in her hair and dress and had a perpetual, quiet smile. Garry took good care of her and she never had to work hard. They had all the conveniences in their home and Isabel did not have any gardening or yard work. They had two devoted sons, Denny and Tim, who also looked out for their mom.

Whenever Helen and Martha visited their Grandma Jewel and Grandpa Broussard when they were small, they would sit on their laps. Broussard was not openly affectionate, but enjoyed holding the girls. He had a very long, tough nail on his thumb, and when the girls tried to touch it and feel its strength, he pinched them with it. That was very painful and they did not like it, and surely didn't think it was funny. He never really let them examine the thumbnail.

In the summer the girls liked to visit Pep, an older relative who lived in a small house near their grandparents. A fig tree grew near his house. It was loaded with enormous black figs, which were very sweet. The girls were free to eat all they wanted. Their lips and mouth burned from the milky syrup on the peelings as they bit into the figs, trying to take the peeling off with their teeth. But it was worth it. They had Celeste figs on the plantation, but these giant figs were much better.

Josephine always sent Helen to get the mail at the little fourth-class post office in the plantation store, and to buy small items. Helen had always been responsible, and even at five years of age she could go to the store and remember to buy whatever Josephine needed and bring home the correct change. She almost always had to take Martha with her.

The plantation store never gave a treat, but Gary's mother, Betty, always gave the girls each a cookie or a wine ball when they went to her store about a block's distance from their house in the other direction. The girls loved to go to the small store. The goody case was near the door, full of candy, cookies, and gum. There were peppermint balls the size of the wine balls, and nearly the same shape. Wine balls were a bit more square, purple, and even better than the grape flavor they resembled. Jaw breakers, smaller, round, hard candies of various colors and flavors, occasionally had a small black center and these were most prized. Betty stocked large cookies from a Baton

Rouge cookie company. These cookies were about five inches in diameter and only cost one penny for two! When the girls had a penny to spend, they often chose these cookies. Their mother had taught them the value of money and wise shopping.

Helen had a paint set she loved, and one day she sat on her bed to paint, but got some paint on the white chenille bedspread. Her heart beat fast as she scrubbed at it furiously trying to remove the paint because she knew she would get a whipping. It wouldn't come out and she did get the whipping.

Occasionally Richard took the family to Pierre Part, where they bought boiled crabs. A picnic table was spread with newspaper and they could get messy as they broke open the crab shell and picked out the delicious white meat. Root beer went real well with it. Sometimes they would bring their cane poles, hooks, line, sinkers, and bait to catch perch off the dock. This made for pleasant lifelong memories for the girls.

Richard was smoking when he met Josephine, and had been smoking a long time. Josephine did not mind because it was customary for most men to smoke. Actually, she made his cigarettes for him. Not many people could afford ready-made cigarettes, and there were very few brands. Richard rarely got ready-made cigarettes, so Josephine made his with loose tobacco from a can and cigarette papers. She held a paper in the fingers of one hand and bent it to make a U shape and stuffed tobacco firmly into it. She rolled the paper over the tobacco back and forth with the fingers of both hands to firm up the cigarette, then licked the top edge of the cigarette paper and rolled it completely to form the cigarette and seal it.

One day she heard of a machine that rolled cigarettes. It was a time saver, constructed of metal and leather, so she bought one. First she placed tobacco in the pocket on the leather sheet, licked the edge of a paper, and placed it behind the tobacco. By pushing the lever from front to back, the cigarette was shaped as the leather sheet rolled the paper firmly around the tobacco and sealed the cigarette. Filters had not yet been invented.

Gary's Aunt Marie from next door came over to visit just as Josephine was making Richard's cigarettes. She marveled at the new cigarette rolling contraption.

"I need to tell Lee about this machine. He smokes a lot."

"Yeah, it really makes good firm cigarettes and it's a lot easier than trying to roll them by hand.

"I think if Lee didn't smoke so much he wouldn't be so skinny," Marie said. "I heard that if you smoke you can lose weight or at least not gain more, so it's probably keeping him slim, but he's really too skinny."

Josephine had gained a few pounds and did not want to gain more. When Marie said she heard smoking would cause one to lose weight or keep weight down, Josephine tried smoking. She smoked for two months but she couldn't stand smoking at all and quit. And she didn't lose any weight by smoking either.

When going out to the field in the morning, Richard brought the strong, black, highly sweetened Cajun coffee with him in a small whiskey flask. He carried it in his back pocket where it fit nicely. The coffee lasted all morning. A little went a long way giving an energy boost of caffeine and sugar. Josephine worked with him sometimes, breaking corn or cutting cane. They got up at 4 AM, made the coffee, and got the girls up. Helen and Martha were allowed to drink a little coffee with lots of milk when they were awakened at this hour. Josephine made sandwiches for Richard and herself with her homemade bread and lard smeared on it. It wasn't a balanced meal but it kept them going all day.

Josephine took the girls next door where Marie gave them breakfast and watched them until they caught the bus with Gary. Lee drove the bus so there was no fear they would miss it. The bus left home at 7:00 AM for school, then returned for a shorter route with kids who lived closer to school. In the afternoon, the first run would bring the nearest kids home, then go back for the rest which included Helen and Martha. They usually got home about four-thirty. Martha studied on the bus to save time. Josephine called out the questions before a test and Martha could see how much she learned.

When Jack the dog heard the bus a mile away, he jumped very high at the end of his chain and barked in delightful anticipation of the arrival of Martha. Josephine always knew the kids would soon be home when Jack jumped. Martha loved Jack, but after a quick pat, she went into the house asking for food. Josephine always made them wash their hands as soon as they got inside. She usually had a snack for them. Often she had made bread pudding, much to Martha's pleasure and Helen's disdain. Helen never liked bread pudding. She and Martha had different tastes.

Martha had lifelong problems from eating so much sugar. Too much fruit also affected her. As a child she fought ringworm, and occasional athlete's foot, which the sugar fed. The doctor prescribed ultraviolet treatments for the ringworm and infantigo on her legs. Her Dad fussed at her for going barefoot because all the "old" people believed that the dew of the grass caused athlete's foot. He even took her to the treater who did incantations and prayed over her, finishing with three Signs of the Cross on her forehead without lifting his thumb.

When Martha was twelve years old, she got a fungal infection on her left hand. The only reason she could think of for getting this aliment which got red, itched, caused water bumps and split skin, especially knuckles, was because she had started dusting the erasers at school. It would be years later before she knew for sure it was fungus. Two dermatologists told her she was either allergic to something or had nervous problems and needed antidepressants. She argued with the last one, saying she thought it was fungus because it "grew" in the fall and spring just as some plants did. His response was, "I'm the doctor here. You can do what I say and pay me, or just leave." That was an easy choice. She left. Later, she got fungus of the toenail and asked her family doctor for something. By treating the toenail with oral medication, the hand was healed, and she realized that she knew herself better than the doctors did.

One day Martha asked Josephine, "Mama, why are some people black and some white?"

"I don't know, except God made us that way."

Seeing so many black people on the plantation made Martha sensitive to their issues, and she often said, "black ladies" and "white women" to give them added respect. The majority of their neighbors were black.

Martha still believed in Santa Claus and the Easter Bunny until she was eight years old. Helen had long since known but kept the secret. Perhaps because Martha was in her own little outdoor world and not privy to much grown-up talk that she was so naïve.

Josephine's mother, Jewel, had been having some health issues and was admitted to the Charity Hospital in New Orleans. Richard and Josephine made the long trip with the girls to see her on Easter Day. Jewel was glad to see them, but she looked so frail. It broke Josephine's heart that she could not be there to care for her mother, but knew the other siblings were near and doing all they could for Jewel.

The hospital ward was full of beds with sick people in near proximity to each other. Volunteer groups had brought flowers and baskets of candy to each patient. Martha looked longingly at the large chocolate Easter bunnies at each bedside, and then reality set in. She did not need to discuss it with anyone. She knew the TRUTH. There was no Easter Bunny and no Santa Claus. She also knew that her mom and dad had done the best they could but could not afford to give their girls everything.

Unbeknown to the girls, Jewel's diagnosis was grim. The doctor told her, "You are about two years too late. You have colon cancer."

Josephine, Richard and the girls visited Jewel as much as possible. They devoted more of their visits to her, rather than trying to visit other relatives, but still were not able to go often.

They had been going to an occasional Western movie on Saturdays, but had stopped so they could visit Jewel more. There came a Saturday when Josephine knew that her mother would not last long, and said, "Let's go to the movies today." They went. She wanted her family to have a little enjoyment before the mourning period.

A few days later, Josephine came into the girl's classrooms to pick them up. They were excited to see their mother at school, but soon became somber as they saw the look on her face. As she took them out of school, she told them, "Grandma Jewel is very sick and may be dying and we need to be there with her."

Richard was waiting for them in the car. It was before noon and Josephine had made sandwiches, so they ate on the way.

Jewel was at home attended by Lois and Carol. Josephine went to her mother's bedside, kissed her and told her that she, Richard, and the girls were there. Jewel was awake and could speak, but so weak that she did not speak much. She knew that her time had come, and her family had gathered around her. She had been growing weaker and finally refused to eat or take her medicine. Lois decided to mash a banana and hide her medicine in it, but she would not eat it.

The vigil lasted only a couple of hours. Garry lit a candle; Catholics use a lot of candles. The girls observed all of this, and noted that when the candle burned out, their grandmother drew her last breath. Garry took a mirror and held it near her nose to see if any breath-frost would appear. It did not.

The funeral was three days later and Richard drove his family back to attend. It was the first death and funeral his girls had ever seen.

Josephine had wanted to give her family that one last movie before she began the period of mourning for her mother, during which she wore no bright colors and did not go to the movies. Well, if Josephine wouldn't go, no one else wanted to go either. The girls were not accustomed to a lot of outings and did not mind. Josephine was a real strong woman, and even though she felt the loss deeply, she did not openly cry. She had a matter of fact attitude about life: accept what she could not change.

"Mom, Santa Claus and the Easter Bunny are not real. Is God real?" asked Martha. By now she had attended church eight years, since her birth, and Catechism for two summers.

"I don't know. They say He is."

Whether or not Josephine believed, she still knelt by her bed to pray, and as she wearily dropped into bed each night, her daughters could still hear her say, "Thank you, dear good God, for this good bed."

A beauty shop in Napoleonville got a revolutionary new machine which gave a permanent hair wave. This contraption looked like something from a science fiction movie. It permed the hair by electricity. Josephine was very adventurous to submit to this process.

First the hair was shampooed and put on rollers. The waving solution was then applied, and Josephine was seated under the machine. Many wires came down from an overhead dome two feet in circumference. Each wire had a clamp which went on a rolled curl. Then, Gina, the hairdresser and owner, turned on the machine. The electricity generated heat which processed the perm. It seemed an eternity as Josephine sat captive to this machine, but the results were worth it. She wound up with a curly head of hair that was easy to maintain and lasted until her hair grew out. She liked to just wet it slightly, comb it, and she was good to go.

Helen had easily manageable hair and had a knack and interest in beauty. She was a natural in all aspects of grooming and rolled her hair in bobby pin curls. They had no rollers at that time. She occasionally played hairdresser to Martha and did an amazing job, but poor Martha had fine textured hair with a mind of its own. When the humidity was high, which was nearly always in south Louisiana, it was very limp. And even with a perm it never looked good. No wonder Richard constantly told her, "Mar-tess, go comb that hair." He had a problem pronouncing Martha, or perhaps he just created a nickname for her. Regardless, that's how he always pronounced her name, and no one ever corrected him.

Gel, mousse, and hair spray had not been invented yet, so it wasn't long before Martha was also getting the electric wave. Gina had a daughter named Rosie, who was just a year or two younger than Martha. She was plump and pimply, and loved to chew bubble gum and blow large bubbles. Rosie didn't hold a conversation well, but she continually tried to talk to Martha while standing in front of her with her nose just inches away. She gleefully blew and popped large bubbles repeatedly in Martha's face while she was helplessly imprisoned by the rollers and wires of the machine. Martha had always been assigned the role of entertaining younger children while the parents visited and she remembered her mother's admonitions to always be nice, so she endured the assault of bubble gum and saliva as Josephine and Gina ignored Rosie's actions. To Gina, allowing this behavior at least kept Rosie out of *her* hair for a long time.

Martha's (grown out) electric wave wearing dress Josephine made

In a few years, home permanents were developed, and Josephine permed Martha's hair. They had a strong ammonia smell, which almost made Martha faint; but it was still an improvement over the electric perm, and cost less. The rollers looked like a drumstick bone, about three inches long, and one-fourth inch thick with a groove on each end. The hair was shampooed, wet with waving lotion, and rolled on the "bone" with a paper to hold the stray hairs in place. A rubber band stretched from one groove on the roller across the rolled hair to the other groove to hold the curl in place. This made for a very curly, sometimes kinky perm.

New items were coming to stores and Josephine was willing to try them. Store bought was the *in* thing. Artificial butter was invented, called margarine, using oil rather than butter cream. The dairy industry was upset and their protest resulted in the consumer having to "make" their own margarine rather than having it already prepared. All ingredients came in an enclosed plastic bag, with a yellow color capsule inside. The homemaker had to manipulate the bag by hand to break the capsule and blend the color into the other ingredients. The girls begged to see which one of them would be allowed to "make" butter until the new wore off. After awhile the process grew tedious, but to Josephine it was easier than taking the cream from the milk to make butter. The girls liked to hear her reminisce about how Garry sneaked in to spoon the cream off the milk and eat it. He still liked to do it even after he was grown.

Josephine bought a two burner kerosene stove, a great improvement over the wood stove. It also had a small oven. No need to build a fire ahead to warm the stove anymore; just turn the handle and apply the match.

Store bought white bread was readily available now, and a grocery store in town sold day-old sliced bread for five cents for a long loaf. When the family was in town, they sometimes came home with ten loaves.

Whenever they were out of bread and not going into town soon, Helen brought a loaf home on the school bus. She may not have liked to do it, but she never argued or made a fuss about how embarrassing it was to bring bread on the bus. Josephine made lots of bread pudding for Martha. She creamed together eggs and sugar, added vanilla, milk, and raisins, then put the broken up bread into it, letting it soak a few minutes while the oven heated. Then she buttered the baking dish, poured in the pudding and topped it with chunks of butter.

While at Lehman's Department Store, Josephine found a real *electric* toaster. It was shiny metal with a door on each side. Each door opened downward by a little wooden knob on the side of the door. A slice of bread was placed on the open door. When the door was closed, the toast leaned on the wires and heat from the element toasted that side. When the door was opened again, the bread slid down the door and flipped so the other side got toasted when the door was closed again. What technology!

Martha was in the third grade when her teacher, trying to teach nutrition, asked all her students what they ate for breakfast. When Martha was asked, her reply was, "Bread, jelly and milk."

"That's not a balanced meal," said the teacher.

Martha was somewhat embarrassed to hear this, wanting to be perfect, and answered, "But it was *toast* bread."

Another gadget Josephine got was a hand held egg beater. It was made of a light metal, either tin or aluminum, and had beater blades much like the modern ones of today. The center held the gears which turned the beaters as the handle on the side was turned. Her left hand held the metal across the top of the gadget as her right hand turned the gear handle.

Divinity fudge and double boiler frostings were now easier to make, and anything light could be beaten easily. Josephine never used it for her cake batter; she continued to cream the butter and sugar by hand to perfection.

Merchants in Donaldsonville began to offer premiums to customers such as a piece of glassware, silverware, or dishes for a purchase of groceries or other merchandise. Some stores and most gas stations offered stamps instead. For every ten cents spent, the merchant gave one stamp. The stamps had to be pasted into small books, and when the books were filled, they could be redeemed for various types of merchandise. When a large amount of stamps had been collected, Josephine and the girls got out the stamps. Rather than licking all that glue, Josephine pressed the stamps against a wet towel and then glued them into the books. Laundry detergent boxes contained bath towels. Glasses were packed in oatmeal boxes as a gift with the purchase of oatmeal.

Josephine always found time to spend with her girls, whether it was sitting on the floor with them doing exercise, playing cards, or reading to them. She had begun to get romance magazines and she sometimes read an interesting story to Richard and the girls.

Ever since the girls could walk well, Josephine took them fishing behind the levee which was just across the gravel road. The Mississippi River was about a mile away from the levee, but they called the bar (borrow) pit the river. This was a channel dug out for dirt to make the levee, and the resulting channel filled with water. So this "river" was only the distance of two city blocks. The girls got the shovel and dug worms when they were old enough. The area where the dishwater was thrown out the window was always moist and provided nourishment for the worms. The trio took their cane poles, the worms in a tin can, and a bucket with them to the river. Josephine taught them how to prepare the hook for the fish. She placed a worm in her palm and slapped it between her hands to kill it, then took a tiny piece and put it on the end of the hook. The topper was when she spit on it for luck.

They were thrilled to catch tiny perch, which were few and far between. When the fish nibbled, it caused the cork to bobble a bit. Tiny fish just ate the bait off the hook without getting caught. If the fish was bigger, he pulled the cork under. Often, some of the black people fished there, too, and sometimes they caught a catfish, or a larger perch.

Josephine and the girls eventually caught a few small fish, but turtles or eels swallowed the hook far too often and they were not appreciated. They were dangerous--turtles and eels could bite--and the eels were slimy. As they twisted about, they covered the line with a thick white mucous no one wanted to touch. Josephine always cooked the perch for the girls, frying it crispy so that even the fins of the tiny fish could be eaten. About ten years later, someone with a casting rod and artificial bait caught some large bass in the same place. Helen and Martha debated whether large bass were there all the time and would have responded to a large wiggly worm rather than the poor bit of worm they offered to them.

In May and June dewberries and black berries ripened. Josephine made jams and jellies and mashed berries with sugar for the girls as a quick snack. They wore rubber boots to pick berries along the ditches for fear of snakes.

June and July were the months when the fig crop ripened. Josephine and the girls picked figs to sell to the canning factory, and preserved some, cooking them with sugar, and processing them in sealed jars in a boiling water bath.

September brought the first of the pecan crop, and when storms came, the ground was covered with them. Josephine and the girls picked all they could. Helen and Martha were allowed to keep the money they made so they could have spending money at the State Fair in Donaldsonville. The school allowed them a day to go to the fair because it was considered educational. They encouraged the kids to view all the exhibits: livestock, baking, canning, sewing, etc. The girls did do that, but they could also go to the rides and games, see the fat and bearded ladies, and hear the vendors bark out their wares. The school bus brought the kids to town and back as usual on fair day. Josephine always admonished them to spend their money on food and rides and not waste it on games and merchandise.

Martha's playmate from next door, Gary, continued to come over to play until Martha was twelve years old. After that age, kids of the opposite sex did not play together. When school was in session they saw each other on the bus, but not much otherwise. They had spent summers together and now both secretly missed the companionship of the other. Martha had taken him for granted all those years. He was *Gary*, her friend, not a romantic interest. Then why did she miss him so much?

It was near Halloween when Marie came over to tell Richard and Josephine that Lee was in the hospital in Donaldsonville. He had been coughing up blood and the diagnosis was lung cancer. Richard took the family to the hospital to see him several times before he died. The girls were saddened to see him in this condition. It was evident that one lung had already been removed, since one side of his chest was hollow, and his breathing was labored. He was matter of fact and did not bewail his fate. They were sorry for him and his brother and sister, James and Marie, and for Gary, his nephew, and his family. Cigarette smoking had not yet been determined to cause cancer. James took over his school bus route.

When Martha was twenty she learned that Gary had been ill and died in the hospital across the street from where she worked. She lamented that she had not known, and did not have a chance to visit him. But at that time she had not met the Lord Jesus Christ yet and did not have the words of eternal life to give either Gary or his uncle Lee: "YOU MUST BE BORN AGAIN."

8

Adjusting to Change

The field work was getting to be too much for Richard, and he bought a new tractor. It was delivered for a payment of $796.37, which was one-third down. Richard kept the tractor next to his car in the barn-garage. As usual, he kept it in meticulous condition, cleaned and polished. The tractor made farming much easier, but he still kept Charlie to plow the garden, and do other things. Richard could also charge Mr. Turner for the use of the tractor when he worked as overseer. Josephine kept the records of this time and usage.

In the coldest part of winter, Richard brought neighbors over to help butcher a hog. The Cajuns called this a bucherie. Josephine and the girls helped as much as they could. The hog was held down on a table constructed of saw horses with boards. Martha's job was to hold the pan under the hog's throat to catch the blood as its throat was slit.

All of the work was done out of doors. Scalding water was poured over the dead animal to clean it and open the pores. The men shaved its skin with sharp knives to remove the hair and then cut the hog open from the neck down, disemboweled it, and cut it in pieces. One of Josephine's jobs was to wash the entrails clean to be used for stuffing sausage. That was the only type of casing available at the time.

The men cut the skin off the carcass with about one and a half inches of fat attached to make pork rinds, (pig skins, or cracklin', as it is called). The fat was scored down to the skin to make for better frying and the cracklin' was cut into pieces about two inches square. They put the pieces in a large black iron kettle half full of water. A fire kindled under the kettle brought the water to a slow boil until much of the fat melted, and the water evaporated out of the pot. The resulting hot fat browned the cracklin' and made them crisp and tasty. The fire had to be stoked with wood and kept at a constant medium-high heat to continue a slow boil. When the fully cooked cracklin' were dipped out with large slotted spoons on brown paper to drain, salt was sprinkled on.

Before electricity, large crocks held raw meat, heavily salted to prevent spoiling, but now Josephine had a chest freezer. They still salted some pork and made sausage and *boudin*, a savory Cajun treat made with ground boiled pork, green onions, hot pepper, garlic and cooked rice. Red sausage could be made by adding the blood to the sausage.

Both the sausage and the boudin were made and stuffed by hand into the clean intestines by use of a metal funnel. The meat from the hog's head, and some of the skin, all chopped fine, was cooked with shallots, garlic and other seasonings to make *hog's head cheese*. In cooking, it became a bit gelatinous and when poured out to cool in a square pan, it became very firm and transparent. It was then sliced into thin pieces, often eaten in a sandwich. The feet, also shaved, were cooked and pickled. Pickled pig's feet were a delicacy.

There was a saying, "Everything on the pig is used except the squeal." Ah, living the country life!

In spring, Richard planted a crop of Easter Lilies. They grew beautifully, but the market was not good, and he didn't make money on that crop. But the girls delighted in the field of flowers with delicate beauty and rich fragrance.

Richard continued to plant corn and cane, the main crops at that time, and still supervised and worked Mr. Turner's crops. He and Josephine planted sweet potatoes, red Irish potatoes, and peanuts, as well as basic vegetables in their own garden. Fire ants had not yet invaded America so that was one pest they did not have to deal with in farming. Josephine was still selling some vegetables and sewing for the local women, most of whom were black. She had a lot of word of mouth business since she did such a good job and did not overcharge.

Richard's brother, Reed, started taking his teenage daughters to the dance in Pancourtville about twenty-five miles away. He enjoyed having a beer and talking to people as the young folks danced and flirted. The dances started at five o'clock in the afternoon on Saturday and could last until midnight; however, since it was a long way to drive on gravel roads at night, he always tried to get them home by ten. On foggy nights, when condensation made the windshield fog up, he would lean close to the windshield to peer through it as he continually wiped it with a towel.

Lots of school kids went to the dance, as well as people of all ages. Some of the same teenagers who rode the bus and lived near Reed's and Richard's family also started going. Helen learned about it soon, and since she was a very attractive girl, some of the boys told her, "Helen, your cousins are going to the dance, why don't you go with them? I sure would like to dance with you."

"Well, I live quite a bit farther and my folks can't drive me, so I don't know."

With all the talk around school and on the bus, Jackie said, "Helen, if you'd like to go with us, come spend the night. You could just drop off the bus at my house on Friday and come with us, and when Aunt Phene, Uncle Bae-Bae and Martha go to church on Sunday, they can pick you up."

"Wow, thank you, are you sure Uncle Reed won't mind?"

"No, I know he and Mom wouldn't mind."

Reed's wife, Helen's Aunt Alice, did not care to go with them and she was used to having a lot of kids around, so one more didn't matter to her. Josephine and Richard had no problem with Helen going with Reed and his daughters. Helen continued to go to the dance with them and in a year or so, Richard and Josephine also went to dances in various places, taking the girls. Martha was thirteen at that time and big for her age. Even though beer and hard liquor were served, there were no fights or trouble of any kind. If there were laws against minors in places that sold liquor, nobody cared, especially minors accompanied by adults.

People of all ages went to dance and hear the music, much of which was country, blues, or jazz. Fats Domino frequently played at the dances. He was enormously popular even though he was young and just starting his career. *Blueberry Hill* and *Hello, Josephine, How Do You Do?* were two of his most popular songs.

Many times the dance halls also sold food. The specialty at one place was turtle stew, a rare delicacy and highly sought. Richard and Josephine went early to be sure to get some.

Josephine was occasionally asked to dance. Richard, of course, still had a balance problem and was content to sit, have a beer or soda pop and watch while Josephine danced. He was never jealous and had no reason to be. Once in a while a strong young woman friend coaxed him to dance a short dance. The oldest person at the dances was an old woman who always had her scarf tied up around her head. Rumor was she was bald under that scarf. She looked very old, as did her skinny partner. Their dancing belied their age, because they could really cut a rug. There were dance halls in several of the nearby towns, and this old couple could be seen at all of them.

Josephine made each of her girls a skirt to use with starched crinolines which puffed out like the hoop skirts of a bygone era. The skirts had six horizontal panels, each one gathered on top and sewn to the straight bottom of the one above. The results were skirts so wide that they could be laid on the floor and spread out around the waist band flat in a large circle. There was quite a bit of sewing involved in making these skirts. The girls liked to make them twirl out wide when they spun around dancing.

No matter whether or not the family had been dancing on Saturday night, Richard still took them to Mass at the Catholic Church on Sunday. In Martha's experience, the only requirements of the Catholic Church were regular attendance, confessing sins to the priest and taking communion. Confessing to drinking, dancing and smoking were not things she confessed.

Not too long after, the church started having a Mass on Saturday at five PM as well as on Sunday. Martha thought it was so that party goers could sleep late on Sunday.

Farming did not pay much so Josephine took a job with one of the local families to help make ends meet. She cooked, did laundry, cleaned the house, ironed, etc. The lady of the house sewed and threw scraps of material and thread on the floor all day.

The youngest child, Junior, was a boy, and highly regarded because he would carry on the family name. The oldest child, Megan, a girl, was quiet. However, perhaps to stand out, the middle child, Chloe, another girl, had a mean streak, and was crafty. She hit Josephine's daughters when they played where no adults were around. Helen and Martha had been taught not to hit, and they didn't go tell the girl's mother, just endured it. Chloe would play nice and then take the girls off guard and then hit them with flag sticks or other objects.

Chloe learned that Josephine had an ingrown toenail and she took great delight in stomping it every chance she got, and laughed with devilish glee as Josephine cried out in pain. As she did with the girls, Chloe struck unexpectedly while Josephine was working.

Josephine never saw her employer discipline her children. She kept the job a few months, then quit. She already had enough work to do at home.

The summer that she was fourteen, Helen got a job in Mr. Turner's fig canning factory. One night she came home after dark when her parents and Martha were already in bed. Since it was so hard to heat water and wash in a washbasin, she just dipped a washcloth into the basin to wash her face and arms, then went to bed. During the night, the girls woke to find themselves and the bed covered with ants. Josephine made a big deal over this. "Helen, look what you did; you got ants all over the bed and your little sister." Helen had got the fig syrup in her hair and that's what the ants were after.

Helen smarted from the reprimand and thought of all the times she had to sleep with a little sister that wet the bed. Josephine didn't do much fussing then. Helen thought, "But Martha is her *baby.*"

The following summer, Martha joined Helen working at the fig factory. They were assigned to label cans that had been filled with preserved figs. Martha took a case of twenty-four cans from a stack, and turned the case upside down on the table to dump them out. Then she lined the labels face down, with each of the short edges about one-fourth inch from the other until there were about fifteen labels lined up with edges exposed. She dipped a toothbrush in paste to spread across the edges of the labels, so only that edge got glue on it. A can of figs was placed on the other end of the label and the can was rolled over the top label and the glued edge sealed down to complete the labeling of the can.

With all twenty-four cans labeled and returned to the box, she sealed the top flaps of the box with the paste, and glued a label on the side of the box. After it was placed on the stack of labeled cases, the job was complete, *for three cents.* Then the process was repeated. On Martha's first day she labeled seven cases and made twenty-one cents. She got a little better over time. One black lady was so fast that Mr. Turner paid her twenty-five cents an hour. The thing was, she could have earned more if she had been paid by the case. No, Mr. Turner still did not discriminate. He paid everybody the same rate for the same work, whether it was man, woman or child, black or white.

Everybody brought their own lunch to the factory, and the most favorite lunch of all was a sandwich of fried baloney with mustard, a marshmallow cookie, and a bottle of pop.

Mr. Turner recruited Helen and Martha to do a special project after they had worked a couple of summers. It was to label jars of preserves. The jars had to be removed and replaced in the box one by one to prevent breakage, and each label had to be laid down and glue applied on the entire label before it was carefully placed on the jar. Since this required more work and care, Helen coaxed Martha to ask Mr. Turner for more money. As he drove them to the factory in his truck, Helen prodded Martha with an elbow in the side. Martha got up her courage and asked, "Mr. Turner, jars are a lot harder to label than cans, so can you pay us more money?"

"You'll... be... satisfied..., Martha.... You'll... be... satisfied," he said in his clipped way of talking. When payday came, the girls got--*three cents a case.*

When Josephine sent the girls to pick up the mail one day, the postmistress, Mrs. Turner, daughter in law of the plantation owner, told Helen, "Tell your mother I'd like to talk to her whenever she has time. It's important."

"Okay, Mrs. Turner, I'll tell her."

"Thank you. Bye."

The girls hurried home and excitedly told Josephine about Mrs. Turner's request and gave her the mail.

"I wonder what Laura wants to talk to me about. I'll go see her tomorrow while she's at the post office. Look, it's a letter from your Aunt Carol. Let's see what she wrote."

The letter began: Dear Phene, I have some good news. I met this really nice, good looking man. He's so polite and everyone likes him. He works at the hardware store in Houma and has a nice car. We've been sweet on each other for a while. He came to visit the other day and asked me to marry him. Dad is going to be okay by himself. I want to get out of this house. Dad has worked me in the fields long enough so I told Maurice I'd marry him. He was excited and asked how soon. I said as soon as you want. It doesn't matter what kind of wedding; I can't wait, but if y'all could come, I'd be so happy. I'll let you know when it is. Lois is happy for me, too. She and Andy are doing fine, and the two children are eight and ten years old. It will be so good to see you. Everybody sends their love, we miss you. Love, Carol

P.S. T-Brou eloped with a girl he met recently. We really like her.

"Hey, girls, Aunt Carol is getting married, and Uncle T-Brou already got married. I can't wait to tell your daddy. We're going to a wedding."

The next day, Josephine went to talk to Laura Turner.

"Hello, Laura, how're you? What did you want to talk to me about?"

"Hey, Josephine, I know you are a real smart woman and I want to give you this wonderful opportunity. I'm resigning from the post office and I think you would do great as the new postmistress. Would you take the job?"

"Well, I don't know. I'll have to think about it."

"I'd show you everything and there are manuals you could read. It's not hard. You already know everybody around here and the store is open all the time, so you'd never be by yourself."

The post office was a tiny room inside the plantation store. Laura's husband had been managing the store and a young man named Stevie worked there whom Helen and Martha knew. He and his sister also went to the dances, and lived a few miles past Reed's house. They rode the bus and went to the same public school in Donaldsonville that Helen and Martha did.

"Thank you, Laura, I'll talk to Richard about it and get back to you."

Josephine went into the store to talk to Stevie.

"Hello, Stevie, how are you?"

"Fine, Mrs. Robert, and you?"

"Fine. Look, Stevie, how do you like working here?"

"I like it real well, why?"

"Well, keep it between you and me, but Mrs. Turner offered me the postmistress job and I'm not sure what to do. I haven't talked to Richard yet."

"Oh, Mrs. Robert, I know you would do just fine and I would help you and look out for you any way I can."

"Thank you, Stevie. That's good to know. Please give me a pound of that round cheese. Don't slice it too thin."

She got the cheese, paid him, said goodbye and went home.

Josephine's emotions were excitement and appreciation for the offer, then fear and reluctance. She had a little bit of feeling put upon; having more work and responsibility. She thought when she married an older man that she would be cared for, not that she would be working so hard to take care of others. But with the girls getting older and school costs rising, they could use the money. She knew it had to pay well, or Laura would not be working there. The girls didn't care one way or another if she wanted to work at the post office. Richard, of course, agreed with whatever she wanted to do. Since she was an enterprising woman, she accepted the offer and became postmistress of a fourth class post office. She did well at the job, and the only really nerve-wracking time was trying to make the money balance. If it was even a penny off, it had to be accounted for; you couldn't just throw a penny in. But it beat housekeeping for that family with three kids.

With the better salary, Josephine and Richard decided to shop for a new car. The total price for their 1953 Plymouth after the deluxe option package, plus tax, was $2,573.00. They gave a down payment of $650.00. Helen and Martha were so proud when their daddy and mama drove right up to school in front of all the kids to pick them up. The car had four doors and was a beautiful bronze-brown color with a metallic glitter. The girls were thrilled they could each get in their own door on their side of the car. Oddly enough, Helen wanted to sit behind her mother on the right side. Maybe it was because she could see her daddy better from that side. Richard kept this car polished, too, just as he had always taken good care of his possessions.

That summer Helen moved to downtown Baton Rouge to work and enjoy city life. She rented a room and walked wherever she needed to go. It was safe and everything was convenient. A lot of her dining was at the drug store lunch counter where an entire steak dinner was ninety-nine cents, and a hearty breakfast was thirty-nine cents. Downtown Baton Rouge, with the State Capitol nearby, was the stimulating center for entertainment and shopping, the seat of government for Louisiana, and drew people from miles around. Of course, shopping malls were non-existent in that era. Helen saved up her money then bought really nice clothes on sale which stayed in fashion and looked good for years. She gave her parents some of her earnings every payday and continued to do so all their lives.

Martha missed Helen very much, and now came home to an empty house, so after she got home from school, she often went to the post office and plantation store until Josephine got off work. She liked to talk to Stevie and help sweep or do anything she could to help.

One day in summer she decided to make some cookies while her mother was at work, and dropped the bowl and broke it. She cleaned up the mess, then wrapped a cloth around her hand and walked to the post office. When her mother saw her she said, "What happened to your hand?"

"I cut it."

"Oh, I'm sorry."

"Well, it's better than if I broke a bowl or something."

"Your hand is more important than a bowl."

Martha ripped the cloth from her hand and quickly said, "Mama, I broke one of your bowls." Shades of her rascally Uncle Garry; she got no reprimand.

Josephine continued to work at the post office but Stevie went into the Army. Josephine and Martha wrote to him and sent him chocolate fudge. He answered their letters in his beautiful handwriting, and sent them pictures. He looked very handsome in his Army uniform.

After three or four years, the government closed some fourth class post offices--Josephine's was one of them--and rural mail delivery began. She saved money while she worked, but she still felt loss to have the job taken away.

Richard began to have health problems. Laura's husband, Bruce, operated the store after Stevie went into the Army. When Richard was no longer able to farm, Bruce offered him and Josephine the position of managing the store. They decided to take the job since they knew they couldn't live in the house indefinitely now, with Richard being unable to farm anymore. There was no other way to make a living there. So their combined salary at the store was $100.00 a month and use of the little apartment in the rear of the store. Even in 1958 that was very little to live on.

There were so many things to give up or dispose of with this change: livestock, the barn-garage, large crocks and jars, many tools and numerous items they no longer had room to keep. Without a garden or animals to care for there was less hard outdoor work, but more food to buy.

For the first time, Josephine and Richard had a real sink with running water that drained and didn't have to be thrown out of the window, and real bathtub and an indoor toilet. Martha had an older boyfriend who gave them a television set. Of course, it was black and white, but it was great nevertheless. Martha enjoyed the shows. Buckskin Bill had a kid's show. So what if she was sixteen, she still loved it--*Howdy Doody*, *Truth or Consequences with Bob Barker*, on and on, so many things to see.

"Honey, it's time to make the last payment on the car. Let's go to town and do that," Josephine told Richard.

"Okay, Cher, let me wash up and change and I'll get the car."

Richard and Josephine were exuberant as they drove into town to pay the balance of the car note at the auto dealership. They left with the paid-in-full receipt and were even more jubilant as they drove out of town.

"Watch out!"

A cane truck had crossed over into their lane, and Richard swerved off the road to miss it. Luckily there was a wide shoulder so they didn't go into the ditch. Josephine always helped Richard, reading signs and watching traffic. The truck missed them, but they always remembered that just as they paid the car off, it nearly got wiped out, and them with it. It was like the devil tried to turn a triumph into a tragedy and was out to get them, but they felt God protected them.

After they moved, a hurricane felled the large pecan tree near their old house into the living room-bedroom combination exactly where their bed had been. Since nearly all the hurricanes roared in at night, they would have been in bed and would have been killed. God spared them again. Luckily, no one was living in the house.

The gravel road was blacktopped. So goes progress.

9

Good Times-Hard Times

It was a new experience running a store, but together Josephine and Richard did it. Store hours were long and tedious, but they closed early on Saturday and were closed on Sunday. It was a large store and the ordering, stocking and cleaning proved to be a big job.

The Plantation Store exemplified what the song *Sixteen Tons* spoke about when it said, "I owe my soul to the company store." People who worked on the plantation were able to put anything on their charge account; however, by the time they made a payday, they often owed more than they drew. It kept them in debt and obligated. It was hard to climb out.

Many times, plantation black men came to their apartment for liquor or cigarettes after the store closed for the day. Richard always accommodated their needs by going to get what they wanted. The buying and selling fell on Josephine since Richard couldn't read or write, but he was always there to help wherever he could. If Josephine took a break, he could get the items someone wanted and remember to tell Josephine exactly what it was so she could put it on their charge account. He was also an extremely good cook and excellent housekeeper.

A friend from their childhood came to the plantation to find Richard. He asked for Bae-Bae. No one knew for whom he was looking, but finally it was decided that he wanted Richard, who was embarrassed that "baby" name was used.

Before moving to the store, Martha asked her Mom if she could take her Dad's gun to hunt squirrels in the pecan groves. She told her to go ask her daddy. Martha found him and said, "Daddy, I want to take your gun and go hunt squirrels. Mom said it was okay with her if it's okay with you."

"Well, if Mama says so, it's okay with me."

Martha was familiar with his single shot, four-ten shotgun. She had seen him shoot squirrels in the pecan trees in the yard, and had often handled the gun, fetching it for him. She knew it was always loaded and handled it with care. Richard always said, "Don't ever point it at anything you don't want to shoot."

Josephine and Martha knew how to skin and clean squirrels and rabbits, and Josephine *really* knew how to cook them, whether fried, stewed, or in a jambalaya.

When Richard said okay, Martha got the gun and a couple of shells and went sit under a pecan tree in the pasture. Soon a squirrel moved toward her and jumped into the tree above her. She put the gun to her shoulder and pointed the muzzle. She followed him with it until he finally moved on. Her heart beat fast and she could not pull the trigger. This scenario continued with four more squirrels, and she went home empty handed. This was her first hunting trip. She was fourteen years old.

When she was sixteen, her boyfriend, Frank, coaxed her to go hunting with him, and the first thing she shot was a 'possum. After that, when a 'possum went after their chickens at night, Richard sent Martha to dispatch the 'possum. She soon became a pretty good squirrel hunter, too. All the folks on the plantation knew her since she was a baby, and were aware when she went hunting alone.

Now while living at the apartment in the store, her parents went to the dance on Saturday nights, but she stayed home because Frank didn't want her going out without him, even if it was with her parents. The black men of the plantation came to ask Richard for something after the store was closed, but they never came to ask Martha to get them anything when they knew she was alone. They told her parents, "I would never go ask Miss Martha for anything; she'd shoot me with her gun."

Martha was sure they were joking, because they liked her, but she was grateful that they had respect for her and her parents in that they did not come around when she was alone.

Frank was quite a lot older than Martha and at seventeen; Martha announced to her parents that she wanted to quit school to get married. She thought Frank would give her a comfortable life since he made good money: *the same take me away Prince Charming thing* that Josephine had thought when she got married. Josephine and Richard did not like the fact that he was so much older and he was somewhat controlling and could manipulate Martha.

"Cher, how can we get her to quit seeing Frank?" asked Richard. "He doesn't want her to go to the dance with us on Saturday night, and who knows what *he* is doing while she sits home alone."

"Well, you know, if we make a fuss or forbid her to see him, it will just make her want to quit school to be with him," Josephine responded. "The girls have their own life to live and have to make their own decisions." Actually, Martha was easily persuaded.

So when Martha asked to quit school, her mom and dad said, "Not many on either side of the family have graduated from high school. We want you to stay in school and graduate, too."

With that encouragement and direction, she did graduate. Her grades in the eleventh and twelfth grades dropped a bit because of Frank, but she still finished as Salutatorian of the class. However, all her classmates and teachers knew the situation of her older boyfriend, and even though she received four year scholarships to two Louisiana universities, no one spoke to her about attending college, and so she didn't. She did go off with Frank after graduating, eventually married him and had many adventures, but hers was not a Cinderella life either.

Helen and Martha visited their parents often, trying to coincide their visits to see each other, too, and went to church, the dance, and bingo with them. Well, Martha couldn't go to the dance; Frank didn't approve. There was always a safe, welcoming and comforting feeling to be in their parents' home.

One day while sitting on the porch at the store, Richard got up to check Helen's car. He found the oil was low. "Mar-tess, go get Helen a can of oil for her car. Tell Mama to pay for it."

"*Dad!* Helen's sitting right here. She could go get it." Her Dad didn't even respond to that, and Martha went in, got the oil and helped her dad. Richard had taught Martha to drive the 1953 Plymouth with it's stick shift, but Helen's boyfriend taught her to drive a car with an automatic shift. Helen thought getting a boyfriend to teach her would be simpler, especially after Josephine ran over the steps of their old house.

The old store still had the square, red cold drink icebox with hinged lids on top. Chunks of ice floated in water to keep the bottles icy-cold. The cash register was a grand, majestic machine with four vertical rows of buttons to key in the price, which showed in the window at the top. A handle on the side opened the cash drawer when turned.

Half of the store had been sectioned off, and the unused portion held about a dozen slot machines which had been moved there when gambling was abolished. Eventually, the sheriff came out to pick up the machines and take them to town.

A black family named Lucien lived about five miles from Josephine and Richard. This large family was well educated, worked on a plantation and ran a school bus route. Some of them played music at all the local churches and dance halls. The whole family was well known and respected by all.

The patriarch invented the first cane cutter, which revolutionized cane farming, and put a lot of farm hands out of work. Prior to his invention, sugarcane was cut with a cane knife. Josephine had cut cane with Richard and her sister, Carol, cut cane for their father. First the stalk was cut at the ground, and then the top was trimmed. The stalks were piled together in bundles and fire was set to burn away the leaves after all the cane was cut in that area, so they didn't have to walk in the black, smutty soot.

Mr. Lucien's new machine very swiftly cut cane, trimmed the leaves off and piled the cane in bundles. He was known for his invention, but later at his funeral, when all his accomplishments were told, it became known that he had never gained monetarily for his invention, because someone else filed the patent on it.

Josephine and Richard continued to operate the store for a couple of years after Martha graduated, then Mr. Turner's son decided to take it back.

"Cher, what can we do? I can't farm anymore and there's nothing else to do here," lamented Richard.

"We'll have to move out. And we need to have some income, so we'll have to go someplace where I can get a job," Josephine said.

Richard had been ill a long time. Dr. Mosley diagnosed him with prostate trouble. Richard had problems passing urine and had to go frequently. The diagnosis and this treatment had continued for many years, but time would prove the doctor misdiagnosed the ailment.

Josephine and Richard searched for a house to rent in White Castle, which had two drug stores, and several grocery and clothing stores, three doctors, a dentist and churches. They found a house to rent within walking distance to stores, although Richard could still drive. The house was in disrepair and needed extensive cleaning, because it had been vacant a long time. They cleaned, repaired and made the house as livable as they could.

Josephine soon got a job at a five and dime. She did not like the job very much, because most of the work was dumped on her; however, she did not have any choice but to make the best of it. She was not very skilled in negotiating fair treatment. Richard did most of the housekeeping and cooking. They made a few friends in the town and visited back and forth.

Josephine, Richard and Martha (rent house on right, 1953 Plymouth behind them)

Josephine and Richard went to dances, bingo, and visited family as usual. They were still in love and made the best of everything and took life as it came.

One of the best friends they found was Mrs. Blanchard. She really liked them and gave helpful advice and information about the area. She and her husband lived in the next town, Plaquemine, where the American Legion bingo games were held.

About a year after Josephine and Richard were in the rent house, the landlord told them they would have to move: his son needed the house. They found another place to rent and clean up, and again were put out of the house when it was in better shape to rent. They'd had a lot of hard times in their lives, but this seemed so *wrong*.

"Honey, Mrs. Blanchard told me at bingo of a little house for sale across the street from her in Plaquemine. Let's go see it."

"Let's go," said Richard. With great excitement they quickly dressed in their best to look at a house they might be able to own, where no one could take over and make them move.

Mrs. Blanchard was happy to call the owner to show it to the couple. They felt that the house was a good deal, and it was nice to have such a good friends across the street to orient them to the area. The asking price was $7000.00 and with a down payment, the house note was affordable. It was a little two bedroom, one bath shotgun house with a hall from the living room past the bedrooms and bath to the kitchen with screened porches on the front and the rear.

Josephine and Richard's house in Plaquemine

There was no air conditioner, and when Helen bought them one, they said they didn't like the cold air blowing on them and wouldn't use it.

Josephine's habits died hard. Rather than use the hot water faucet, she continued to heat water on the stove to do dishes and washed them in a dishpan in the sink. She threw the water out the back door. All this was done to save utilities, she said. Martha told her living like that was like camping out.

The washing machine was put in the garage, because the kitchen was so small. There was no place for a dryer, and no 220 wiring for one, so clothes were hung on the line to dry.

Josephine and Richard were able to plant a garden on the land behind their house, and it wasn't long until Josephine had a fig tree growing in her yard. She and the next door neighbor, Mr. Taylor, shared vegetables with each other. To Josephine, working in her garden was like an escape, a tranquil time to think.

Plaquemine was a very noisy town. Randy Lear, the neighbor on the other side, repaired lawnmowers and ran them full throttle all day. Numerous dogs throughout town often set up a roar of barking, especially when the wailing toots of trains on the tracks blasted at all the crossings, which were numerous. Trains traversed up to six times a day and the tracks were only a block away from Josephine's house.

Mr. Blanchard died a year later, but Mrs. Blanchard continued to be a great blessing to them. When Richard was sick, she drove them to the doctor, and took Josephine to the store. She visited often and sometimes brought something she had cooked. She was Italian and a great cook. Martha found her personality a little overbearing and grating, but soon learned that it was just her way; she had a good heart and really was a good neighbor to her parents.

Helen continued to send her folks money, and after she got married to Mike, a wonderful man, she was able to give them more. Mike liked to give his mother-in-law money to play bingo, or to buy something for herself. He nicknamed Josephine *Mama Bear* and Richard *Papa Bear,* because their last name, Robert, was pronounced Row-bear. Josephine and Richard adored him. People of all ages or cultures loved Mike. He and Helen had a great and loving relationship and didn't mind showing affection in public, holding hands and kissing. They often fussed and picked at each other openly. When Martha first heard them fuss, Helen laughed at her stricken face and said, "Don't take it so seriously, we're just playing."

Mike moved the unused air conditioner into the guest bedroom so he and Helen could be comfortable when they visited the folks. He also did some carpentry work to make the house more energy efficient.

Josephine sent cards to her daughters and their husbands on their birthdays and always sent money with it, usually $5.00. Helen continued to send money to her parents often, and sometimes when shopping for herself, she bought a purse, shirt, shoes or other item to send to her mother or father.

Martha was heartbroken when Helen and Mike moved out of state. One night Josephine dreamed that Helen was in a bad part of a big city and was frightened for her. Later, Helen wrote that she had been apartment hunting and found herself in a scary situation in a bad part of town. So again that premonition kind of dream happened. After saving their money and renting a few years, Helen and Mike bought a house. Martha was devastated, and knew she and her sister would never live close to each other again.

Josephine and Richard were happy to have their own home. Nobody could make them move again. Josephine was able to walk to grocery stores, and to work. She worked at a grocery store, then later at a clothing store.

The grocery store allowed people who worked there to help themselves to cold cuts and other food, and Josephine joined the other employees in snacks, the frequency of which caused her to gain weight. She went on her own diet, cutting out bread and sugar, and eating meat, rice, potatoes, and vegetables of all kinds. Soon she was back to her normal weight.

Richard received Social Security Disability in 1961. He continued to be ill and their savings were being slowly depleted. He was still going to Dr. Mosley in White Castle. They had respect for the medical profession and did everything the doctor told them. His resistance was low, and a really bad case of shingles covered his entire torso with sores. It was very painful, with a tormenting itch aggravated by heat or cold. The doctor said shingles was often caused by a re-activation of the Chicken Pox virus dormant in the spine, when a person's immune system is weak from illness or stress.

After he recovered from shingles, blood was found in his urine, and still Dr. Mosley did not find the cause. Finally, when the bleeding continued and nothing would stop it, the doctor sent him to Our Lady of the Lake Hospital in Baton Rouge. By the grace of God, a wonderful urologist, Dr. Hargrave, correctly diagnosed bladder cancer within an hour of his admittance.

Both daughters and Josephine were by his side as he was treated there. They rented a room nearby and took turns staying with him. About three fourths of Richard's bladder was removed in surgery. Whenever he had to leave his room for tests or surgery, he said, "Cher, hold my watch." Josephine kept his watch, eyeglasses, dentures, and wallet. That became a ritual as treatment continued.

The doctor gave him three years to live. But soon an invention allowed scraping of the bladder by means of a cystascope. He was to return every nine months to have tumors scraped out of his bladder. After five years he was declared cancer free. The doctor applauded

Josephine, Helen and Martha for being there and encouraging Richard. He said family support played a major part in a patient's recovery. All the operations wiped out Josephine's savings, but she was able to pay all the bills.

Josephine took over more of the heavier work as years went by. Richard did not have the strength and stamina he had when he was younger and healthier. She painted, put putty on the window panes, mowed the lawn and gardened, as well as working at a job. Now, her brothers and sisters really emphasized, "Phene has a hard life." They also said poor Richard suffered a lot in his life.

They went crawfishing sometimes, and often to bingo, dances, and church. Richard was still able to drive. Soon he had to have the tip of his earlobe removed because of cancer, and also the tip of his thumb. It was bone cancer. He still cooked and did dishes, but losing part of the thumb made everything difficult. He could no longer peel pecans.

Josephine always told the truth and if asked to color the truth, she refused. She was tactful, but outspoken when angered. At the bingo hall, there was additional betting on the bingo games. They called it betting on the horses. People could place bets on a number from one to fifteen, and as the bingo game progressed, whichever number had all the numbers under it called and lit up first was the winner. Josephine began to have very good luck picking the winning number. She picked thirteen and a woman noticed how often she won on it, and bought up all the thirteens. Josephine was so angry that she told the woman, "I hope that number never comes out." She must have put a hex on it, because it was several months before thirteen ever won again.

Martha's husband, Frank, was well liked by men, women, and children. He could always get a job and make good money, but he was prone to quit a job just to go off fishing or hunting, so they never got ahead. It was like paddling a boat in the wind. When you quit rowing, you start being blown back. Many times they were broke. It seemed at these times Martha would get a letter from Josephine with a five dollar bill just in time to buy some groceries. Josephine had no way of knowing when Martha needed it. It must have been Mother's instinct, but the money always arrived when desperately needed. Whenever they got a paycheck, Martha would send five dollars back to her mother. Martha worked a waitress job sometimes, but with

Frank wanting to move often, she could not get a good, permanent job.

Richard and Josephine celebrated their 39th Anniversary in 1974, and years later Josephine said it was the happiest they had ever been. He was about sixty-five and Josephine about fifty-five. Helen and Mike sent Josephine and Richard a beautiful card for this 39th anniversary, and Josephine kept it all her life.

Eventually Richard became sick again. He knew he could not drive safely now, and Mr. Joubert, who owned the service station had been telling Richard that if he ever wanted to sell his 1953 Plymouth that he would be happy to buy it and would take very good care of it. Richard hated losing the independence and sense of manhood he had with his car, although he knew he had to sell it. But it was a source of pleasure whenever his girls told him they saw Mr. Joubert drive the car and it looked great.

Richard was seeing Dr. Dupree in Plaquemine now. Josephine had to help Richard walk down the hall from the bed to the kitchen. Martha came home from out of state and when she saw the condition her dad was in, she told her mother that he looked like a dying man. The doctor was giving him vitamin B shots every week and taking weekly urine samples, but had not given a diagnosis. So Martha went in to talk to the doctor herself, bringing the urine sample. His response to her questions was, "Don't rock the boat."

"If that had been the attitude seventeen years ago, my dad would have died."

"Well, maybe that would have been a blessing."

That is all he would say. Martha told her mother and Josephine said, "When the doctor last came to visit he talked with me on the back steps and said, *'Mrs. Robert, you have a hard row to hoe'.*"

Martha talked to her dad without saying anything about what the doctor had said. She asked him, "Dad, do you feel like you're real sick or is it that you just don't feel like walking?"

"Well, I guess I don't feel like it."

"Dad, do you think you could have tumors of the bladder again?"

"No, I would know if I had tumors."

Martha called her sister and told her what had transpired, and that she believed her dad was deathly ill, but was not able to convince anyone to do anything. Helen got on the first bus to go see for herself. When she arrived, her dad assured her he was okay. Mike fussed at Martha for upsetting his wife for nothing. Mike never got angry at Martha, but now he phoned her saying, "Don't you ever call my wife and upset her like that again."

Three months later, Richard got another doctor, Dr. Michaels. This doctor diagnosed leukemia, *advanced* leukemia.

They did give him a pill form of chemotherapy, but treatment for leukemia at that time was not very successful. He was admitted to the local hospital a few times for blood transfusions. Every time he was admitted he had to get a chest X-Ray again, even if it was only two weeks apart--hospital rules. It was very painful for him to be moved from bed to bed for the X-Rays.

A young black nurse, Angela, who knew his situation, and that Richard did not have much family to donate blood, told Richard that she would donate blood for him. Martha had just donated some, and when this precious little nurse offered, tears welled in his eyes as he looked with gratitude at her and thanked her profusely. Kindness such as this always brought him to tears. Angela promptly gave blood for Richard.

As his illness progressed, Josephine quit her job to care for him. Toward the end he got a hospital bed, and Josephine did everything for him, except for once a week when a nurse came in to do a checkup and bathe him. That was all the relief Josephine had. Martha visited frequently to help with shopping and errands, but the bathing and cleaning of Richard was Josephine's responsibility. And she seldom got a chance to leave the house.

Martha drove Josephine when she had to leave the house for any reason. They really tried not to leave him alone, but when they did, Martha asked Randy LeBlanc next door to watch out for Richard since he was bedridden.

By this time Richard was very weak. He began to have bedsores in spite of the lambskin he lay upon. His tongue broke out in sores and chewing was not an option. Josephine and Martha fed him baby food. In all of this misery and pain, Richard did not complain.

Helen came to spend the last two weeks of Richard's life with them. She did the cooking and most of the cleaning, and was staying with them night and day. Martha worked a new job, but came every afternoon. Having Helen there to help was a great relief for Josephine. Richard asked his children if they thought he was being punished for something because he was ill, maybe for shooting the varmits that ate their chickens. The best wisdom they had at this time was no, they did not believe that. Richard had all three of his girls with him when he passed away.

Josephine held up well through the funeral, making all the decisions with the girls. Martha's husband, Frank, and Helen's husband, Mike, were at the funeral. Helen was grieved to lose her father and never did well at funerals. She clung to her husband for comfort. Martha was stronger and was able to interact with the family and visitors.

Richard had three flower arrangements: one for his casket, one from his niece, Jackie and her husband, and one from the chemical plant where Frank worked. All the guys working with Frank took up a collection for Josephine. Martha was very touched at that.

After the funeral, Josephine's sister, Lois, asked her if she wanted to move near her to be with her blood relatives, but she said no, she wanted to stay in her house. Helen also asked her to move in with her; Josephine gave her the same answer.

Martha wrote to Dr. Hargrave after Richard died. She thanked him for healing Richard from bladder tumors and giving them eighteen more years with him.

His response came on a Thank-You card: "I'm glad I could do it, but it's the wonderful support of the families that make the difference, and I appreciate that y'all were always there for Richard during his hospital stays."

Josephine was so drained from Richard's illness that the girls felt she did not need the stress of trying to get a job: what she needed was rest. She was too young, by about four years, to draw a widow's benefit of Social Security. It was determined that she could live on $150.00 a month, so every month Helen and Martha each sent her $75.00. Helen was used to sending her money and always sent a little more. Josephine's brother and sisters still sent her a little every once in a while. Josephine's house was paid for and she was accustomed to conserving everything. Now Martha lived close by, visited her mother often, and took her shopping and to visit her family.

Two months after Richard died, in April, Martha took Josephine crawfishing. They gathered the poles, net, bait and bucket, and brought the big washtub, driving west on U.S. 190 out of Port Allen until they found roadside ditches with plenty of water. The crawfish were medium-sized, hungry, and so plentiful that they filled the washtub half full. This was the highlight of Josephine's life at that time.

Crawfish trying to wiggle through the net

A middle aged woman named Sally and her family moved in across the street. Josephine gained another wonderful neighbor and friend, who took her shopping between the times that Martha came and helped her in many ways. Josephine missed Richard a lot, but as always, she took life as it came and made the best of it. She had a wonderful attitude of gratitude for a home, food, family, and friends.

10

Rejoining Society

During the mourning period of two years, Josephine adjusted to being alone because she was in her own home, the first and only one of her very own, that she had shared with her faithful Richard. She reminisced with Martha of their 39th Wedding Anniversary, which was the best of all. They had their own home, albeit small and primitive, were enjoying life, and though Richard was never well, he had not been really sick since the bladder cancer years ago.

That anniversary marked the happiest time of their lives. Josephine held the picture of her and Richard taken a year before he died. They were sitting side by side and he had his arm around her, with his hand falling over her shoulder displaying the thumb that had been cut off at the first joint because of cancer. But they were both smiling with love and happiness. Any feelings she sometimes had of the hard work and circumstances were gone now that she was alone.

The man who bought Richard's 1953 Plymouth valued it and kept it in the same excellent condition that Richard had. Martha, Helen, and Josephine saw him drive it around town every once in a while. They were glad to see the car. It brought back happy memories, and they knew that Richard's car was cared for.

Memories can only console one so long, and Josephine began to want to go out and mingle with others again. When visiting Jill, (Dan had died three years before Richard), Jill talked about some friends who were going to a dance hall a few miles from her house. Josephine knew some of these people, and had played bingo with them in the past, so she wanted to get back into the swing of things. Jill invited Josephine to stay at her house and go to the dance, so she did. Jill did not dance and did not want to continue to go regularly, but Martha took Josephine a couple of times. A nice looking man named Lonnie became interested in Josephine. Martha liked him and thought he would be good for her mother.

Lonnie continued to be interested in Josephine, but competition set in! Another man, Tyrone, and his girlfriend, Elizabeth, whom Josephine knew from bingo, were there at the dance. Tyrone was nicknamed Ty for short. Ty began to show interest in Josephine who really liked Ty better than Lonnie, but until Elizabeth challenged her with, "You ain't woman enough to take my man," Josephine had kept her distance. But now the gauntlet had been thrown down. The taunt and dare made Josephine's feminine wiles rise up, and it wasn't long before Ty and Josephine were an item. They had a strong chemistry between them. Ty lived in Plaquemine also and a new romance began.

Ty was a generous man who liked to go to the mall, restaurants, bingo, and dances, so they had a great time. Josephine was happy with the attention. Martha still visited a lot and got along fine with Ty. She would have preferred it to be Lonnie, but you can't fight physical attraction and the dare from Elizabeth.

Ty was very overweight, had high blood pressure, and wasn't very active. Josephine had always performed outdoor activities, and this continued. Ty tried to help with repairs and such, but many times Josephine did not want to change things. One thing she asked him to do was to block the wind from blowing under her house. Her house had no insulation except that Mike lowered the ceilings from nine feet to eight feet and put insulation between the original beaded board ceiling and the new acoustical ceiling he had installed for Josephine and Richard when they first bought the house. He also put paneling over the beaded board walls. That didn't improve insulation value very much, and there was no insulation on the tongue and groove pine floor either, just the single boards. Any time the temperature dropped to 50 degrees with these little frame houses on piers, it was bone chilling despite the gas space heaters. So Ty put boards around the bottom of the house. It also kept cats and dogs and other animals from bumping around underneath. Richard would have known better than to block all ventilation under the house, but if Ty knew, he did it anyway; he just wanted to please Josephine.

They went to the Catholic Church and Martha and Helen went with them whenever they were visiting. In addition to Sunday morning services, the church now held Mass on Saturdays at four PM or five PM depending on the season. So they attended on Saturday, then they all went to the bingo hall following church. Ty liked to sit in the back of the church. Martha teased him and said it was because he wanted to make a quick getaway.

Helen and Mike were still living out of state. Mike had three teenage children from a previous marriage, a mother, and lots of brothers and sisters to visit. He always took Helen to Josephine's first then he visited all his family.

Josephine loved to make him chocolate pecan fudge or her chocolate pecan cake. He was her favorite son-in-law, more like a son. She loved him because he made Helen happy, and he'd always rave over everything, "Mama Bear, you make the best cake, and the fudge is just like I like it. Here's ten dollars for bingo."

During the time shortly after meeting Ty, Martha got a mutual agreement divorce from her first husband, Frank, and soon met Martin. Everyone called Martin Mr. Wonderful. He was friendly and helpful, funny and outgoing. Martha and Martin got married in that same year. They remained in Louisiana two more years until

Martin took an early retirement, and then they moved to Florida, near Daytona Beach.

Josephine cooks in her kitchen with Martha

Helen and Mike arranged for Josephine and Ty to visit them at their home, and took them on trips a few times. They all enjoyed that.

After Martha and Martin were settled in Florida, they also wanted Josephine and Ty to visit them so they could show them local attractions. Josephine and Ty flew from Baton Rouge to Orlando, where Martha and Martin met them.

There was so much to do at the theme parks that the men couldn't keep up. They preferred sitting in a coffee shop, so the women split from them. Josephine and Martha saw shows, rode the rides, and ate sweet treats.

When they reunited with the men, Martin took lots of pictures of them in the theme park. One was of Josephine and Ty hugging face to face. She was delighted with it all.

Martin and Martha slept in their travel trailer so Josephine and Ty could stay in the larger mobile home. Martha showed Josephine how to adjust the thermostat if they got cold. In the morning Martin told Martha, "Ty is sorry you showed your mom the thermostat because he felt like he was baking all night, she made it so hot". Josephine had always hated drafts and for her feet and head to be cold.

Josephine wore a kerchief everywhere. Before they left Daytona, they drove to the beach, where more pictures were taken to record the trip. Josephine stood in the ocean breeze with an exhilarated look on her face. She wore no kerchief in that picture.

Whenever Martha visited them, Ty took Josephine and her to visit the family in Labadieville and Thibodaux where some resided. He liked to tease Eileen, Richard's sister, and Jill, Josephine's sister, both of whom soon had to go to a nursing home. They liked the attention

Ty gave them because he was so funny. Eileen, still very particular, instructed the nurse exactly where to place her shoes or other items in the closet or drawer. Josephine and Martha always brought her bananas. She did not like them too ripe. Martha liked to visit relatives with them because Josephine could translate French, and Ty would make jokes and tease them and make everyone laugh. It passed the time. After they left, Ty always said he never wanted to be put in a nursing home.

Josephine never married Ty because her girls were afraid if she would leave her house to go with him, she would lose her home and be homeless if it didn't work out. Josephine was getting a little Social Security after she turned sixty, about $200.00 a month, and would have had more married to Ty, but in the end, she did the right thing to stay where she was. Things had cooled down some between her and Ty.

As time passed, Ty stayed at her house more and more and let his own house get in disrepair. When a hard freeze came and the water pipes burst, he just shut the water off. Later, his neighborhood became filled with crime. Someone stole his boat and motor from his back yard. None of the neighbors would get involved if they witnessed a crime. Ty used to go fishing frequently with a friend until the theft.

Ty went downtown every day to visit his old work buddies, and often brought home plate lunches from the supermarket or other places with to-go lunches. He did not care for the Cajun style foods Josephine prepared, especially since she cooked lots of vegetables and low fat dishes.

Ty and Josephine still visited Eileen and Jill in the nursing home. Martha went with them whenever she could. Jill was obese and had diabetes. One of her godchildren, Lillie Bell, had taken her in and cared for her as long as she could before Jill went to the nursing home.

Jill gave the nurses money to buy her candy--not a very good thing for a diabetic. After being there about a year, Jill had one leg amputated above the knee because of diabetes, resulting in her becoming bedridden. Before that, even being obese, she was able to get in a wheelchair to go to the recreation room and visit others. She was very likable and social, so now it was hard on her emotionally and physically.

Martha and Martin were in Florida a year and a half and Martha was taking Community College courses when Martin said, "I want you to think about where you want to live and build a house because I'm ready to leave Florida. It's too hot here."

They settled on Tennessee hill country and built a sturdy, well insulated house. Whenever Martin didn't need her help with construction, Martha cleared undergrowth of vines and weeds and moved rocks to form a circular drive around a large tree. She also helped drive nails in the floor and with framing the house. When it got too high up, she quit because of fear of heights. Martin bought trusses and hired roofers to install them, the roofing, and the siding.

After getting all settled in, they both got seasonal jobs at a theme park. A friend at the job gave Martha a New Testament bible. As a Catholic she had never had nor read a bible. She read the entire New Testament beginning with the Gospels: Matthew, Mark, Luke, and John. "What's this? They are just repeating the same story over and over." She didn't know the disciples were all telling their version of the same thing. She had no idea what she was reading, except it told of some interesting promises.

They returned to Louisiana to visit his family and hers, and Martha and Josephine visited Jill. During the visit, Martha said, "Nanan Jill, I won't be able to come back and see you until September, when my seasonal job is over. I have to go back to work when I get back to Tennessee."

Jill quietly remarked, "My work is over."

Martha took Josephine home and went back to Martin's family. She and Martin planned to go back to Tennessee the next day when they got the call in the morning that Jill had passed away. So Martin and Martha stayed to attend the funeral.

Josephine told them, "Remember Jill said her work was over? She knew she would be dying and was ready to go."

"Yeah, Mom, it was strange how she said it."

Martha and Martin received a letter from Josephine and Ty following Jill's death. It was the typical newsy letter she always wrote. "Received your letter just as we were leaving to go to Baton Rouge and we were glad to get it. We went visit Rita a while, then we went shopping for a shirt or windbreaker for Ty. It got down to forty-eight degrees this morning. The wind is cold. Yesterday we went pick pecans and then went get a few groceries. Went to Bingo last night but didn't win anything. I picked a few bell peppers and 3 tomatoes and 2 eggplant. There's still flowers on the plants but it is getting too late for them. Winter's coming. I love and miss you. Tell Martin hello. Hope you both are well, Love, Mom and Ty."

Josephine's neighbor, Mr. Taylor, who grew a garden and shared vegetables with Josephine, said his wife was very ill and frail. He always cut some of his eggplants off the vine for Martha to bring when she was going to visit Helen because he knew Helen loved them. He was a good neighbor. Martha loved to converse with him over the fence. His wife was a sweet woman, but after a long illness, she passed away.

Martha was in Tennessee when she got the call that her mother and Ty had been in an accident. They were bruised up a lot and the truck was totaled. They were driving home when a teenage girl ran a red light. The light had not been installed very long, and she just zipped through and hit the truck on the left front fender. The truck had no seat belts, and the crash threw Josephine toward the point of impact. Her head hit the frame of the windshield in the center near the rear view mirror and shattered and pushed out the glass. Her left arm, side, and leg hit the dashboard. Ty had some bruises also because he hit the steering wheel, but since he was already on the side of the impact, he did not fly far.

Martha wanted to go to her Mom and take care of her, so Martin said, "Sure, call your job and ask for a leave of absence."

By the time Martha arrived in Plaquemine, Josephine's wounds were black, and her mother was very despondent. They had been taken to the doctor following the accident. The doctor called the wounds hematoma, because of bleeding under the skin and in the damaged tissue. Her head wound had bled and also got black and blue. The doctor pulled shards of glass from her forehead and face.

Martha took several pictures of Ty, Josephine, and the truck so they could have them for an insurance settlement. The mother of the girl who hit them had insurance coverage, was very sympathetic and sorrowful that her daughter had caused them this pain, and she called every day to ask what she could do. She drove them to the doctor and to the store before Martha got there. Then her insurance company told her to quit communicating with Josephine and told Josephine to quit bothering their client.

Martha answered the phone when the insurance company called. They wanted to talk to Josephine hoping to get a quick settlement. Martha said her mother wasn't up to talking right now, and besides, they needed to see how recovery went. Perhaps she would have trouble years from now because of this accident.

Martha asked a friend of hers, a State Trooper, if he knew a good lawyer. He recommended a young woman whom Martha saw. This lawyer said she couldn't get much in that type of accident. Josephine and Martha decided that $5000.00 would be about all she could get, and advised Ty to talk to his lawyer also. His truck wasn't new but he had new tires and battery. He wound up with $700.00 for his totaled truck and signed the release. Then he found out he was responsible for his own medical bills. He had expected the insurance company to pay them. By accepting the money for the truck he forfeited his right to other expenses.

Martha stayed two weeks and told her mother that when the insurance company called to say she wanted $10,000.00 and maybe they would give her $5,000.00. They did call as soon as Martha left and asked her how much she wanted. She said, "I want $5000.00. I was hurt bad and have pictures to prove it."

They asked her to mail some pictures, and when they received them, they put a check for $5000.00 in the mail immediately. Josephine was satisfied and put the money in the bank. Like she always said, "It's not what you make; it's what you save that counts."

Later, Martha found out that $5000.00 was the minimum expected from any kind of injury, so she felt the lady lawyer did not give very good advice.

Helen and Mike continued to live and work out of state and had a very happy life together. Helen always cooked for him and waited either at the door or outside for him to return home from work or wherever he went. She knew all the little things that made a house a home and made her husband happy. Mike adored Helen. She was very attractive and had always dressed nicely and wore high heels. When Mike pulled into a full-service station to get gasoline, he would have to tell the attendant who cleaned the windows, "Man, are you going to wear out my windshield looking at my wife's legs?"

Helen had always nagged Josephine and Martha to go for yearly check-ups at the doctor and get mammograms and tests. Mike was also nagged into getting check-ups. He was a carpenter and spent several years installing acoustical ceilings made with asbestos. Asbestos was just beginning to be identified with lung cancer. Mike skipped his X-ray one year so the cancer in his lungs had two years to spread to other parts of his body. He took chemotherapy and radium but lost the battle. He died soon after. What a devastating blow to the whole family and to everyone who knew Mike. It really saddened Josephine, not only for the loss she knew Helen faced but her own, too. Mike had always been so good to her.

Helen, like Josephine, wanted to stay in her own home and continue life alone as best as possible. Helen no longer sat in the same chair she used when Mike was alive and also changed bedrooms. When five PM rolled around, she always left the house and went somewhere. That had been their special time together each day and she could not bear it alone at home. One other thing she did, she bought a color TV. As wonderful and generous as Mike was, he accepted change slowly, and stubbornly resisted color TV.

Josephine began to show signs of change, a listlessness of sorts. "Martha, I don't know what's wrong with your mama. I used to take her to the mall and all, and now I can't get her to go anywhere. I told her I'd buy her a new outfit but she doesn't want," Ty told Martha when she visited.

Martha rationalized, "Well, maybe she's just grieving since Mike died. You know she was crazy about him. She'll get over it."

Ty was so concerned that he even called Helen long distance to tell her that her mother had changed.

Three years after moving to Tennessee, Martha received a book called *Power for Living*. It was published and distributed by the DeMoss Foundation in Florida, designed to convert people to Jesus. No religion, just a relationship. She read where God wanted to be in control of her life, and through faith in what Jesus did on the Cross she could give her heart to God. The entire time she was married to Frank, she knew someday she would have to find out what God wanted and do it, so she knelt and prayed as the book suggested, admitted she was a sinner, asked forgiveness and for Jesus to take over her life. It's called being Born of the Spirit, or Born Again.

Martha's doctor in Tennessee practiced a more holistic style of medicine than most. The doctor had business cards which read, "If you meet me and forget me, you've lost nothing, but if you meet Jesus and forget him, you've lost everything."

Martha and Martin rolled their eyes at this and said, "Quack." The doctor told her that he had seen God do miracles. She continued to go to him and strangely enough began to want to go to church again. She visited a Catholic Church in Morristown but knew that wasn't right for her.

One day she told her doctor, and he wrote down the names of three churches he recommended. She called for the service times of two churches and told Martin she was going to one. She said she got the names from the phone book, (since they had thought the doctor a quack because he was so gung-ho on Jesus).

After visiting the first church, she knew God was real and could guide her life. It was a non-denominational, full-gospel church that taught from the King James Bible. She told her family and tried to explain all she learned about God to them without them being offended. Her sister was most outspoken about not wanting to hear about it. Once, though, she did say, "You've changed a lot and become nicer since you married Martin."

Martha answered, "It's not because of Martin, it's because of Jesus." Martha found it easier to write to people about salvation than tell them face to face. Whether they accepted it was between them and God. Martha kept searching for more answers to help change her personality and visited many churches. She began on a good foundation that Jesus bought everything she needed for her mental, physical, spiritual and emotional health on the cross, but the other churches and TV preachers with their prosperity and unity messages took her off course, causing her to rely on works.

Ty began to have small health issues like glaucoma and cataract surgery where the hardened, cloudy lenses of his eyes were removed. He then wore eyeglasses with very thick lens. Soon symptoms of heart trouble surfaced. He was told to lose weight or see another doctor. He was unable or unwilling to lose weight. He had several episodes when Josephine had to call 911 to get paramedics to the house for him. He always got the same orders from the doctor: lose weight.

Josephine had always had good posture, but she started slumping, so Martha nagged her mother to straighten up. She wrote to her from Tennessee, "Mom, raise your hands, praise the Lord, and straighten up. Practice straightening up every day."

One day when Martha was visiting Josephine, Ty asked Martha to go with him to the store. She said OK. Martha got in Ty's car. He got behind the wheel, started the engine and said, "I want to talk to you about something. You know I had a will and my niece was going to get everything, but she died. When my wife died, I made a settlement with my stepdaughters, so I don't owe anybody anything. I want your mom to be taken care of. What do you think I should do?"

"That's nice of you, Ty. I know Mom can use it. Do you have a lawyer you can trust who will do what you ask?"

"Yeah, he'll do what I say."

"Then go talk to him and tell him what you want and get him to make a new will."

"Yeah, I'll do that. Don't worry; your mom will be taken care of."

Helen and Martha always tried to visit their mother and Ty simultaneously so they could see each other, too. Josephine's housekeeping was slipping. She accumulated more things than she had room to store, and Ty had brought a lot of his things into the tiny house. Ty had newspapers everywhere, and left sticky mint and gum wrappers all over the house and in the sofa cushions. He took antacids continually for what seemed like indigestion to him.

Helen and Martha spent an entire day cleaning the living room, taking down the old drapes, and installing blinds. They were tired at the end of the day. Josephine and Ty had stayed in the kitchen, not showing any interest or pleasure in what they had done.

Martha and Helen were going to go back to their motel about eighteen miles away when Martha told Helen, "They act like they just as soon we leave them alone. They don't seem to like what we did. Let's just say goodbye and leave tomorrow without coming back to see them again."

"Okay."

They told Josephine and Ty what they had decided and said their goodbyes. The next morning, Martha had a change of heart and said, "I think we ought to go back and see them again before we leave."

"Yeah, well, *you* were the one who said we should just leave."

So they drove back and found them in church, sitting in the back as usual. Both Josephine and Ty were overjoyed to see them again. They all went to the cafeteria for lunch after Mass and visited awhile before the girls left for their homes in opposite states. It was almost a holy moment; there was so much love in this visit. This was the last time the girls saw Ty alive.

About a month later, Ty called out in the night, "Phene, come here and sit with me in my room. I don't feel too good."

Josephine sat with him a while and asked him if he needed her to call the paramedics. He said no, it wasn't that bad; just sit with him. She sat a long time and he went to sleep, snoring lightly. She went to her own bed and slept. When she woke in the morning she found he had died during the night. She called for the coroner to come, and Ty was taken to the funeral home.

When Martha heard the news, she hoped that all she had told Ty about God had made a difference in his eternal soul. She called her mother to say she'd be there right away. Josephine and Ty's nephews arranged the funeral and burial. No one said anything about a will; there was none in the box of papers Ty had left in Josephine's house. Ty had a military funeral because of his service to his country, and they presented the flag on his coffin to Josephine.

After the funeral Martha went back to her home in Tennessee. Six months later when Martha visited, she went to the court house to see what the will had said. She was told he died intestate. Whether he never changed his will and was called intestate because the heir had died, or if he had written a new will and it was not found, Martha never learned. What she did learn was that the assets he left were divided between his living kinfolks. Josephine got nothing.

11

Martha Comes Home

Josephine again refused to live with her daughters or sisters and remained in her house. Martha and Helen were still out of state, but Josephine had two great neighbors, Sally and Mrs. Futrell, who took her shopping and looked out for her. Josephine continued to grow vegetables, pick figs, and cut her own grass.

Martha loved her life with her husband in Tennessee but kept thinking of her mother getting older and being alone. She thought to herself: here I am raking leaves for an eighty year old woman in Knoxville and my own mom is getting older and having to do it all by herself. She probably has about ten more years to live and I sure would like to be closer to her. Martha was concerned about her mother being alone so she wrote to her Aunt Lois and got this letter back:

Dear Martha and Martin,

We received your sweet letter and were glad to hear from you. You know I will always do whatever I can for your mom. She is my heart. We were always close growing up, doing things like picking berries, cherries, going crabbing in the bayou or crawfishing in the canals. Aunt Carol was the pretty one and she got a lot of attention and flattery. Boys were her big thing at seven or eight year old. Your mom and I just did what came natural for us. We were farm girls. I still like to get in my kitchen, make cake, pies and a big dinner for my five children and Andy. They all had lots of friends so it made for a house full.

Your mom and I were close and she married at sixteen, so you know I missed her, but your dad was a sweet guy and always told me when your mom died he would marry me. Later I found someone of my own so he quit teasing me. When Helen came along that was a great thing for me. I loved to make her talk and do things for her. Then they moved on the river by the time you came along. They always had so much work to do that they only visited for Easter or Christmas. Garry and I would go spend vacation with you and maybe a few days at Christmas.

I am concerned that she is so far from us, but she did put my mind at ease when she told me she had neighbors she could call on. Your mom is so independent and thinks she can live alone. But she didn't steal that trait. Grandpa Broussard was just like that except more independent. I can remember growing up hearing the same phrase, "I don't need no neighbors, I don't need anybody." I did not understand him and I even accused him of not loving his children. He told me yes, he loved his children when they were small and depended on him but after they were grown they were on their own. He had to die before I appreciated that fact. He was born to German ancestors and they never showed him any affection.

No matter how humble her home is, you know she will want to stay there. Your mom seemed to be taking Ty's death as if she expected it, but was still nervous. She seemed so dejected I hated to leave her. All she could say was she was waiting for Martha. I am glad you got there soon after we left and she did go see

Ty that night at the funeral home. He was well fixed and seemed so natural.

I know what you mean when you say the children nag the mom. I saw it with Aunt Carol when she was so sick. The children would try to tell her what was best for her. Your mom will do what she wants. I just pray that God keeps her well enough to care for herself.

Lots of love to you both,

Aunt Lois and Uncle Andy

Lois's letter was a great relief and support for Martha who was experiencing guilt for not being there for her mother. In September, Martha and Martin planned another trip to see his folks, plus Josephine and Helen. To save a few days, they asked Josephine if she would like to go with them to see Helen and Josephine did.

Martin washed and waxed Helen's car and did some carpentry chores at her house in Texas, installing better doors and locks since she was a widow. Josephine just sat around mustering a smile whenever needed. She was not her usual upbeat self. Helen liked to go walk at a little mall so they all went. Martin was never into walking, so he and Josephine just sat on a bench as Helen and Martha walked back and forth. The girls remarked that their mother had lost her competitiveness. Time was when she would have walked right alongside them.

In October, back in Tennessee, Martha kept getting vibes that something was amiss between Martin and her. Conversations were taking an uncomfortable turn and he was on again, off again, warm and cold toward her. Finally he said he wanted a divorce. She had suspected all that past summer that something was going on. At the mall where he worked, a lot of joking and flirting went on among the employees. He also came home late at night, something he had never done, and smelling as fresh as when he left--indicating he had taken a shower--and the socks he removed were not his. Martin insisted there was no one else. All the security guards, including Martin, had started wearing cologne and joking about the "candy store." Martha assumed it meant the kid's clothing store near Security where pretty young girls worked. Then he asked for the divorce.

Martha did some investigating and found out who it was. She was a fat, pretty, blond girl who *did* work at the suspected store. She was thirty years younger than Martin and she had a little boy. Martin was sympathetic about the circumstances she was in. Her live-in boyfriend, the father of her baby, did not contribute much and she had to cook dinner after she had finished long hours at work. Martin also had got tired of Martha's change of attitude since she started going to church. She wasn't any fun anymore and didn't want to do all the things they used to.

Martha could not avoid the divorce and knew that she would have to leave. If she stayed there she could not make a living and would never be able to get away to see her mother and sister. She knew she could not afford to keep the house or maintain it alone. Again, she thought about how she longed to be near her mother, that she may only have ten more years to live but she did not want to have to move because of a divorce! It was unbelievable that Martin would turn her away. It hurt so much she thought she would die. Even with the infidelity, she did not want to leave.

She pondered whether to live near her mother or sister. Her sister was frail and alone but Martha felt her mother needed her more, and she herself could do better back in Louisiana as far as getting a job. When she got legal issues settled she went to her mother's house and put in applications for work then visited her sister awhile. It was in the early nineties and recession had hit the country. Jobs were not easy to find but she did get one in Louisiana.

She attempted to live with her mother, but Josephine did not like air conditioning. Martha went to buy a small window unit, but was told she could not use an extension cord with it. The window in the living room she chose for her room was too far from the plug. She could not stand the hot humid Louisiana weather without air conditioning, so she looked for a used mobile home, found a good one, and after getting new carpet and furniture, it looked great. So her time was spent working at her job, fixing her mobile home, taking her mother shopping, cutting the grass at both homes, painting and repairing Josephine's house, and church--a full Gospel church.

One month after Martha moved into her mobile home, Hurricane Andrew began brewing in the Gulf of Mexico. Martha was working at a furniture store and the boss would not close early or allow his employees to leave early even though they did not have one single customer all day. Martha called her mother and told her to have the lady across the street take her to the shelter; that she would gather supplies and join her when she could.

They spent the night in the shelter, lying on the floor along with a few hundred other people. The Red Cross volunteers provided food and drink. Battery radios provided news of the hurricane's progression, and when day came the wind was still strong but the hurricane had passed. Martha took Josephine to her house where the only damage was torn screen on the front porch and the screen door on the back porch was ripped off.

The electricity was off, but the telephone still operated so they called Helen to tell her the news and Martha left to go to her trailer. All the way there she saw great damage: downed trees and the rest stripped bare of leaves, mobile homes blown off their foundations and roofs ripped off. She said, "God, if there's any damage to my trailer, I am leaving Louisiana." Some trailers had major damage in the trailer park, but hers had received *zero damage.* The only problem was the electricity and phones were out. She was dead tired and just went to bed. Meanwhile, Helen and Josephine worried about her and her trailer, not having heard from her. Martha never thought about how much her sister worried.

The stores where Josephine shopped had not changed, but now she was having trouble finding the peanut butter. "Mom, you know it's always on the second aisle," Martha nagged.

229

Josephine bent over more as she stood and walked. Martha even took pictures of her in hopes it would motivate her to straighten up. One day she asked her mother to stand as straight as she could, and she *did* stand very straight, shoulders back. She could still straighten up, but she continued to bend over as time passed.

The good neighbor who used to share vegetables with Josephine had gotten a little crabby, so they were not getting along well. Martha continued to talk to him over the fence and tried to get them to be friends again but it didn't work. Josephine told Martha how he would stick his tongue out at her and how she stuck her tongue out back at him.

When grocery shopping, Josephine bought a lottery ticket or got Martha to buy it for her if she didn't want to go. Martha's new faith in God kept her from wanting to gamble, but she bought her mother's tickets for her. This continued for a couple of years until Martha asked her, "Mom, how would your life change if you won the lottery?" Josephine pondered this seriously and quit buying tickets. She was content with life as it was.

Lois and Andy sent an invitation to Josephine for their 50th Wedding Anniversary celebration and said to invite Helen and Martha. Helen couldn't go, but Josephine and Martha did. It was a grand party and all Lois' children were proud of their parents. It was a great time of seeing family members that they hadn't seen in a long time and some they had never met.

The tap water was not very good to drink in Plaquemine. It tasted very strongly of well water but at least it was clean. The trailer park in which Martha had bought her used mobile home had rusty water. Everything turned yellow. She had to use products in the washing machine to prevent the rust from staining her clothes too badly. She started going into town to fill gallon jugs with drinking water for herself and Josephine from an outdoor dispensing machine. It cost 25 cents a gallon. This was a tedious chore; sometimes it was raining, or very hot. Martha never got accustomed to the Louisiana heat and humidity. She felt very sorry for herself.

Josephine still did some of her own cooking. She liked to cook chicken breasts, and sweet potatoes smothered down in a little water with butter and sugar until done. She liked boiled Irish potatoes and cooked vegetables from her garden. Her favorite bedtime snack while Ty was alive was ice cream, but now it was a small chunk of cheese and peanut butter on two crackers. She took vitamins religiously. She liked chocolate wafer bars and individual chocolate pies. She still ate mints and antacids as Ty taught her to do but in a couple of years she quit using these; she really didn't need them. Undoubtedly, Ty used them because he did eat wrong, and because he had heart trouble which gave him discomfort that he thought he could relieve with antacids and mints.

Josephine's little garden had gotten smaller, but she wouldn't quit trying and carried water in gallon jugs to water it. Martha tried to help but conditions were no longer good for growing a garden with pollution from nearby chemical plants, overgrowth of trees, who knows what?

Martha still took Josephine to visit her folks and friends. Martha felt more comfortable visiting people with her mom there. It gave her more of a feeling of belonging. Martha was still in disbelief that Martin would divorce her and did not want to have any contact with her. It felt like so much rejection.

Josephine's sister and brother, Lois and Garry, with some of their kids, visited Josephine often. One day Garry remarked to Martha that Josephine used to cook and feed them when they came. Now she didn't even offer, so he went to get fried chicken for everyone.

Martha still did not know the extent of what was happening to her mother and said living with Ty changed everything. He always went out and bought food. But reality was Josephine knew she was not able to cook and serve a big meal anymore, and avoided anything that might give her away. She was still able to hold a conversation and appear normal, so no one knew her growing fear that she was not as capable as she used to be.

12

Old Age or What?

There was not much to do in Plaquemine, but Martha took Josephine out to eat at the local cafe' and fast food places. Josephine retained her great manners and social skills. Sometimes she went to church with Martha. It wasn't the Catholic Church, but Josephine didn't mind, she kind of liked it. She said it reminded her of when Bitsy, the black lady, took her to church with her as a child. And she was glad when anyone spoke to her or hugged her at church.

Josephine still tried to cut her grass herself while Martha was at work, doing a little bit every day for as long as she could. It was thick St. Augustine grass and bogged down the mower if it wasn't cut often. Martha fussed that it didn't look good at different lengths and she cut it all at once. The neighbor, Mrs. Futrell, told Martha about this wonderful black man who cut yards, raked, and did odd jobs. His name was Morris; whether it was his first name or last, Martha never knew. Everyone called him Mr. Tim, and she did, too. He was very tall, over six feet five, and still had a lot of strength and agility. Mrs. Futrell assured her he took care of everything like it was his own. He was very reasonably priced, too, and did a perfect job. Martha was cautious about having strangers near Josephine, but with this recommendation she felt assured.

Josephine did not like having Mr. Tim around at first. She was wary of most strangers, especially men. She wanted Martha to cut the grass. Many times when the grass got a little tall, Martha went to find him and asked if her mother was giving him trouble about cutting the grass. Martha suspected that Josephine sent him away saying, "Martha's going to cut it."

"Oh, no, I'm gonna cut it," and he immediately did. He never would rat on her mom or say unkind things about her. He truly cared about helping an old lady and the middle aged daughter who was struggling to hold it all together.

Martha admired Mr. Tim very much, and tried to be there whenever he came to cut the grass to prevent problems with her mom. He did many repair jobs for them also. Martha scraped and painted the porches, put putty around the window panes to keep them from falling out and anything she knew how to do.

There were plenty of other things Martha needed help with. One day she attempted to repair her mom's outdoor table and bench set. It was very large and heavy. She had managed to turn it over and was wrestling with trying to unscrew rusted old bolts. Mr. Tim was preparing to cut the grass and came over and took the hammer, and with just one swing the bolts broke off. He went with her to the hardware and lumber store to make sure she got the best cypress boards and the right bolts and helped her complete the job. He didn't charge for this extra help. Martha sanded and stained the wood with a nice redwood stain which would help preserve it without peeling.

Helen's step-kids and grandkids were just like blood relatives. They always invited Martha and her mom to functions. It was a lively bunch. Josephine loved the little great-grandchildren. She was crazy about all babies. Everybody--family and Martha's friends--said Josephine was so sweet. But there came a time that Josephine did not want to join them on holidays. She wanted Martha to fix the food and bring it to her house. They'd eat and open presents alone unless Helen was able to come. Helen tried to visit about four times a year and especially liked to go for Josephine's birthday on Christmas Eve and for Christmas, Easter and the Fourth of July. Martha loved the noise and laughter that her little family never had, also the big variety of salads and desserts of a big gathering. Her in-laws always had those big get-togethers. She really felt cheated when her mother wanted them to celebrate alone.

Helen wanted her mother's mind to stay sharp. Ty had gotten home delivery of the Baton Rouge newspaper, so Helen gave her mother money to continue receiving it. She never forgot to send money for the paper. Years ago Josephine bought the paper when LSU played football so she could clip the sports sections to mail to Mike and Helen.

Helen also wanted her mother to get health insurance designed for older people, so Josephine complied. At first it was about forty-five dollars a month, but it increased nearly every year. Josephine complained about it, so when it got over eighty dollars a month, Helen and Martha paid the balance. Josephine also scrimped on electricity. Plaquemine had the highest utility rates anywhere. Al Gore could have made Josephine his Poster Child on conservation of Planet Earth.

Summers were getting hotter, and Josephine got heat rashes. She always was adamant about not getting an air conditioner, but Martha finally convinced her to allow her get an electrician to check out the wiring in the house and add four 120 volt circuits, and two 220 volt circuits. Now they could get air conditioning and in case they wanted an electric stove or dryer later, the house was wired for it.

Martha shopped around and got a large window unit which was an air conditioner and heat pump. It worked by thermostat. It wasn't powerful enough to heat or cool the whole house, but it did make the house more comfortable and took out the excessive humidity. Josephine really didn't have to adjust it, but she kept turning it off.

When Martha went over after work she found Josephine sitting on the back steps in the shade. Josephine complained about her heat rash. Martha kept telling her mother to leave the air conditioner alone; it would keep the right temperature by itself, but she said it got too cold at night. After much fussing by Martha, when Josephine saw Martha drive up, she sometimes would go inside and turn on the air conditioner before opening the door for Martha. Of course, it was obvious that the air conditioner had not been turned on all day until now, especially when the thermometer showed ninety-plus degrees.

One day when Martha went in, the house was a hundred degrees and the air conditioner was running. Josephine said it had been on all along but Martha said, "Mom, the metal legs of the table would be cool, not hot, if this air conditioner had been running a long time. It's putting out cool air from the unit." Martha was losing control and went out on the back porch and let out a scream of frustration so loud that the neighbor came running over saying, "Mrs. Robert, you okay?"

Martha told him she was the one who screamed and why. When he heard the story, he said, "Don't worry, Mrs. Robert, I'm going to come over every day and make sure the air conditioner's on." To show his disapproval, he just ignored Martha and didn't address her at all. Next day, Martha asked Josephine if he came to check on her.

"No, indeed!"

As far as Martha knew, he never did. Martha knew that Josephine's memory was not good but she could see that she was still capable of reasoning. Josephine knew Martha would be angry because she was not using the air conditioner and turned it on when she arrived. So she attributed it to her mom's stubbornness and fear of a large electric bill. The bill was usually fifty or sixty dollars a month, and the girls paid the excess over forty dollars. The conflict over the temperature in the house was frustrating to Martha; in fact, everything was stressful for Martha since she had returned to Louisiana. Having to go into a stifling house to make the grocery list for her mother and clean up the house was nearly unbearable, and trying to make things more comfortable and easy for her mother seemed like a losing battle.

Josephine now left food in the refrigerator until it spoiled. Once Martha had brought her a quart of gumbo, and found it a week later. It had to be thrown out. Josephine picked figs and put them in various containers in the refrigerator. She did give some to neighbors, but many of them just molded.

Martha was taking Josephine for yearly checkups and decided to talk to the doctor beforehand about her suspicions, unbeknown to Josephine. The doctor told Martha that they tested and ruled out any other reasons for memory loss, and if nothing could be found, they called it Alzheimer's. He told Josephine that he had a little test, a questionnaire that the nurse would give her. The test proved that she was losing some mental cognition, but it was still mild. Josephine also had arthritis, and the doctor said she had osteoporosis, but had not done a bone scan. During subsequent years Josephine had three bone scans and they all showed she did not have osteoporosis. Martha always suspected that the head injury in the truck accident led to her memory loss, and that caused her to stoop over, looking like she had osteoporosis.

Josephine had to have a growth removed from an arm and also a mole on her back which proved to be basal cell carcinoma, but they removed it all so she needed no follow up.

Martha began to read everything she could about memory loss and Alzheimer's. She found theories that aluminum poisoning could cause it, about chelation therapy reported to eliminate it, and found a doctor who dealt with such. Josephine used deodorants with aluminum and had cooked with aluminum pots for years. The doctor did a thorough check up and background, then finally at the request of Martha, did take a hair sample to send off to the Smokey Mountain Lab in Tennessee for analysis. It proved negative, so Martha quit grasping at straws, but tried to keep herself informed to deal with the doctors, treatments, and medicines to make sure they were the best for Josephine.

Martha never said the word Alzheimer's to Josephine or in her presence, but used the term memory problems. Josephine knew that she did have such, because she quit doing anything she knew she couldn't do. She once burnt the teakettle when she forgot it on the stove, and never heated water on the stove again. She quit cooking certain things and now got canned chicken. Martha helped her cook her sweet potatoes and other foods. Josephine ate a small portion of several dishes so the cooking only had to be done every few days.

Josephine knew her home and was never the roaming kind or mean like some people became. Everyone always called her sweet. She liked to sit on the glider on her screened porch and talk to the people who walked by. The great neighbor who looked out for her, Mrs. Futrell, checked on her and stood outside the porch to talk to her at length. Josephine never unlocked the screen or invited her in, but did value her friendship. Ever since Ty died, her girls told her to keep her screen door latched and she did.

Andy, Lois' husband died, and Josephine could not stand or walk far, but she insisted she wanted to go to the funeral so they went. It was a long drive from Josephine's home, and after the church ceremony they followed everyone to the graveyard. Josephine just couldn't make it all the way to the grave site, so Martha sat her down and went for the car to pick her up. Josephine, fighting off tears, told everyone, "Andy was always so good to me; I wanted to go to his funeral."

Josephine's house had begun to smell musty so Martha removed the boards around the bottom of the house. She had been telling her mother that they stopped air from circulating under the house. Josephine complained that dogs or animals were bumping around under there, so Martha got some chicken wire and put it around the bottom of the house to keep animals out. Often Josephine still thought she heard something.

There were changes at work and Martha hated change. Actually, she was a great worker if it was routine, but the stress of learning something new and the fast progression of technology and computer programs was difficult for her. She was not a great typist either, and many times it was the favor of her co-workers and bosses that got her through. It was not always so, and she had to change jobs a couple of times. Also, trying to help her mother was always on her mind.

A great break for Martha occurred when she applied for work at a state government agency. She went straight to the human resources division and introduced herself and left an application. The next day she received a call to interview for a clerical position. When she arrived for the interview, she was led to a small cubicle where she met a black woman with a light complexion. On the wall was a poster saying, "Watch out; I can be a witch." Martha was uncomfortable just reading it. The woman's name was Kathy. Martha was told her duties and they hit it off fine. Before Kathy offered the job, she asked, "Do you think you can work for me?" She meant, can a white woman work for a black woman ten years younger? Martha looked at the poster and said, "Well, that poster says you can be a witch, but I don't believe it."

Kathy laughed heartily and Martha got the job. Two days later when Martha was introduced to Kathy's boss, they discovered they had been born within two miles of each other. Kathy was the daughter of the man who invented the cane harvester, Mr. Lucien.

Kathy was a good boss, and many of the others also commiserated with Martha's plight to help her mother. A really great help was a very classy young lady who was secretary to the entire section of accountants. Letty was a proficient typist, and kept time records as well as many other tasks. At times, she had to help Martha with her typing, because Martha really needed help. Letty had a knack of doing her work while people came up to her desk to chat. Her gaze of rapt attention while they talked caused them to pour their hearts out. Never once did she say, just go away.

One day in spring when Martha arrived at Josephine's house, her mother said she saw some bugs in the living room. They were termites. Undoubtedly, closing off the bottom of the house with boards trapped the dampness from the ground making it moist and dark, just what termites love. Martha called a local termite company and they sprayed the house. Martha and Josephine bought a contract and asked how they would know if future damage was caused prior to spraying. He said they would inspect every year and spray if necessary. Their inspection consisted of opening the cabinet under the sink and looking in it. After another couple of years, Martha and Josephine saw termites in the spring, and the inspections of just looking under the sink continued. They kept telling her there must be a water leak in the house to provide the termites with moisture. They would not acknowledge that the termites could be traveling to and from the ground into the house.

Josephine continued to receive letters and cards from her family and friends and she always tried to remember to send some to them also. She always sent her daughters birthday and Christmas cards with five dollars in them. Gradually she was not able to remember and sometimes forgot Martha's. Martha never said anything, but always made sure that Josephine sent a card to Helen. And with that supervision, Josephine always remembered to put the money into the envelope.

One Mother's Day, she received a card from Helen. The printed material said, "Thank you for all the beautiful memories that I will always treasure. Each day gives me a greater appreciation for everything that you've taught me, and for that I am grateful."

She wrote in her own hand, "Dear Mom, I'm sorry I won't be with you for Mother's Day but I'll see you soon, God willing. (Josephine and Helen always said

God willing,) I hope you will have a wonderful day. Maybe Martha will be able to take you out to eat with the money. I love you and Martha. Your daughter, Helen."

Martha did take Josephine to a Mother's Day buffet with the money Helen sent. There they sampled ham, turkey, fish stuffed with crabmeat, mashed potatoes, dressing, milk, cake and peaches. Josephine enjoyed the Mother's Day outing very much, but two hours later she could not remember what they ate.

Martha gave Josephine a home permanent. Josephine had always liked her hair very short and curly. This perm came out that way and Martha thought: it's a shame to make your mama's hair this short and curly. So this was the last perm she gave her. She learned that her mother had good hair. It was salt and pepper gray, but very shiny and beautiful. She began taking her to her own hairdresser. Amy loved Josephine and told Martha, "You're right, you don't have good hair; but your mother has great hair."

Since Martha's divorce, she wrote to her ex-husband's aunts and mother. They wrote or sent a card at least once a year. They were trying to discourage Martha and trying to say give it up, your marriage is over, but they loved her and she loved them. She did manage to take her Mom to see them every year or so.

The three aunts all died a couple of years apart, until there was only his mother left, and two in-laws. At that time she wrote to Martha and Josephine saying, "How the mighty have fallen." It was never expected that she would outlive the rest of her siblings. She was the one with diabetes. She said it hadn't been a good year for her, being hospitalized with congested lungs and serious anemia. She needed multiple blood transfusions and said they couldn't find where the blood was going. She wrote, "I don't mean to be a Gloomy Gus because as long as I can see and hear from my family and friends, life is still worth living."

Martha's ex husband, Martin, lived with his mother to care for her and keep her out of a nursing home. (He had left his new young wife after three years of marriage.) Martha called and asked him if she and her mom could visit his mother. She said, "I'd like to see her while she's alive, not in a coffin." It was early December. He said, "Of course."

When they went, they had a nice visit, cordial with Martin and loving with his mother. Martha had always written people since she became born again telling them how to get saved, so again she told the lady the story how Adam had sinned and caused the entire human race to be under the curse of sin. The penalty of sin is death. A Holy God cannot fellowship with sinful man, and only the death of a sinless man, Jesus, could pay the price of our redemption when we confess we are sinners and accept Jesus as our Saviour. The old lady said, "If only it was that easy." Martha said, "It is!" She died three weeks later. Martha went to the funeral service, but not the burial. It was time to let the family have their last goodbye. Martin never called her to see how her own mother was doing, and Martha never tried to contact him again.

Josephine still tried to make her grocery list and was doing a good job, but Martha noticed that she wasn't getting antacids anymore, and she never asked for more vitamins. She still went to the grocery store with Martha, but leaned heavily on the grocery cart using it to support herself.

She started letting her house clutter up and lined the hall with cans of juice that her good neighbor, Sally, who worked at the food bank, gave her. Josephine never wasted anything but wasn't using it all. After a couple of years in such a hot house, when Martha convinced her to let her clean up the hall and see if the juices were still good, they weren't. The solids had settled to the bottom and the liquid was thin and sour. Josephine hated to throw anything away.

Josephine started "losing" the keys to her freezer (which was on the back porch), and to her chiffarobe. Every once in awhile, the chiffarobe key would mysteriously appear, then disappear again. Other things disappeared. Martha bought extra combs, bobbie pins, safety pins, wash cloths, etc. for her mother. She gradually tried to de-clutter the house, but she didn't go through her mother's bedroom. All the while, Josephine was putting the towels and things in drawers or places where she had never kept them before. She had the towels in with the lovely quilts she had made as a young girl, the most beautiful one being the Little Dutch Girl quilt with colorful hats and dresses on the Dutch girls.

Josephine started losing weight and when asked why, she said she didn't want to get fat. Martha saw cereal bowls on the table and other dishes when she came over after work. She learned that Josephine was leaving the dishes on the table, and when she saw them, she thought she had already eaten, or she just forgot to eat.

Martha always washed the dishes and cleaned the house when she was there. Her mother's skin was very dry from so many years in the sun. One day while sweeping the bedroom, Martha said, "Mom, what is all this white stuff on the floor by your bed?"

"I don't know."

Martha learned that Josephine was sitting on the bed, rubbing and scratching off the dead skin from her legs. Her lips were splitting open, also. Martha thought it was fever blisters. When they would not get well, she took Josephine to the dermatologist who gave her a salve for the fever blisters, and advised using a special brand of lubricating soap and lotion for her dry skin. Martha did not live with her and was at work all day so she could not see to it that she used the products. The lips continued to split. Martha realized that Josephine did not have fever blisters, but chapped lips, so she wrote Josephine notes to apply lip balm. Josephine had always loved to read, and now every time she saw the note, she put on lip balm and her lips got better.

When Josephine got her Social Security check, she always sent Martha to the little bank to cash it for her. Progress moved forward with great leaps causing the government to insist on direct deposit. Martha argued with the bank at length. She thought Josephine might not understand the change. Everyone at the bank knew them but it did no good against government regulations. So she had to tell her mother that she would not be getting the check in the mail and they had to fill out forms for direct deposit.

Josephine seldom wanted to go shopping so Martha picked things up for her and was paid back. Sometimes she forgot, but Martha rarely reminded her. Now, Martha got a little purse and withdrew two hundred dollars at a time to buy her mother's things and pay her bills. She made sure that Josephine had at least twenty dollars if she wanted to send the teenager across the street for something during the day. Martha kept a record of the purchases and the balance in a notebook, and when the money ran out, she withdrew another two hundred dollars.

Martha tried to tell her sister, aunts, and uncles that Josephine's memory was very bad. They wouldn't believe it and said, "Everybody forgets something when they get old. I forget things myself."

When they visited relatives, Josephine still had social skills and did not have to perform, so no one could see it, not even Helen--until she visited and spent the day with Josephine while Martha was at work. Helen asked her if she would like a sausage biscuit from town and she said yes. Helen drove to get them and when she offered one to her mom, she said, "I don't want that." She had forgotten she said she wanted one. This was a big shock to Helen.

One day Martha went for a sausage biscuit for Josephine, since she thought it was a big hit when Helen brought them. She gave it to Josephine who sat on the front porch on her glider, then went to the kitchen and promptly returned to her mother on the porch. "Mom, where is your sausage biscuit? Did you eat it already?"

"Well, I guess so."

"What happened to the wrapper?"

"I don't know."

It took a long while to find the sausage biscuit because Josephine had been sitting on it; luckily it was still in the wrapper.

Martha wondered how she could best care for her mother. She knew that Josephine loved her own home and did not want to leave it. Martha was sure that as long as she was there, she would never roam. And there was the wonderful Mrs. Futrell to look in on her often. She could see Josephine on her front porch from her house.

Martha had tried to make the house as comfortable as possible, but now the floor was starting to give way. The termite company had sold out to a larger company. They refused to acknowledge wrongdoing and said there must be a water leak in the house. Mr. Tim went to the lumber company with Martha and chose replacement boards, fixed the floor joists in the bathroom and the floor, replaced the tile, and reseated the commode with a new wax seal. In the living room, when removing rotted boards he saw live termites. Martha put them in a jar but they soon died.

Martha's boss said to call the Louisiana Pest Control Board, who gave her the same spiel the termite company had, but did come to inspect and found trails up the piers allowing the termites to come in and out. He made the termite company come back and trench around each pier and treat the house again. That ended the infestation, but they would not pay for repairs. Eventually, the kitchen and porch floors also started to deteriorate from the damage. This house needed too much work and nothing short of stripping it down to bare frame would help.

Martha constantly prayed, asking God for a solution. Every door seemed closed to her. She had always prayed for a miracle for her sister since the doctor had told her he had seen miracles, now she was praying for a miracle to heal her mother's mind. Martha cried a lot.

Martha wrote a letter to her mom but never gave it to her. She realized that it was more for herself than Josephine. She wrote:

Dear Mama,

I'm glad you came to spend two nights with me. I know there are some unspoken things between us, about how you worry about your future, and mine and Helen's. I know you don't like being a burden and try to keep things from worrying me. Like when you get confused even in your own house, about how much help you really need and are not getting. About how lonesome you are. I've tried to figure out the best for you but still don't have the answers. The day will come when changes will have to be made.

It's been a rough seven years in Louisiana for me, but I'm glad I have this time to be close, to mourn our lost youth and vitality, and to laugh together over silly things, to love.

Please forgive me for all the times I nagged, yelled and cried. I didn't understand it all. I know sometimes you were stubborn, most times you just didn't know, or were not able to do certain things. I'm very proud of you, and so grateful for all you did for me, for letting us go and live our own lives, for all your wisdom, hard work and ethics. You are so very sweet and dear to me. I can't tell you how much I love you. I can only try to show you. Someday we'll all be together in Heaven and it will be glorious. We'll remember all the good and forget all the bad and be in the love of God which is so much greater than any love we've known on earth. Martha

Josephine now called Martha at odd hours. She answered saying, "What's the matter, Mom?

"Nothing, I just wanted to see how you are."

"Mom, it's four AM."

"Oh, it is? I'm sorry. Go back to sleep."

One night Martha had a dream that she, Helen, and her mom were going shopping. Josephine and Helen were walking ahead, with Martha trying to catch up to them so she could show them what they were looking for. She called out and Josephine turned, radiant looking, tall, healthy, smiling with red lips, high rosy cheeks, and beautiful black hair, just like when she was young. She had happiness, confidence and love in her eyes. Beyond her, Martha could see Helen looking at merchandise on a table. When Helen was told of her dream, she said she had a similar dream of their mother being young and vibrant. Although it wasn't reality, it gave them a comforting feeling to see her that beautiful, loving and competent, and the memory remained with them in following years. Maybe it was a longing for how things used to be with their mother. Anyway, to Martha, it was the gift of the blessed hope of Heaven to come. Jesus is the Blessed Hope; He is the only Way to the Father and eternal life.

13

God's Help through People

Josephine no longer wrote to anyone. Not much mail arrived at her house either, so Martha wrote and mailed this card:

Dear Mama,

I just wanted to make sure you got some mail, so I grabbed this card. While I'm sending it, I'll just take this opportunity to say I love you. Thank you for being such a good mother. We always appreciated how you never nagged or meddled.

I remember how you were such a hard worker and a real entrepreneur. You still are; the way you always had of making extra money, picking and selling pecans, sewing, vegetable gardening, etc. Hope you get this by Saturday. Have a nice weekend. Love, Martha YOU TAUGHT US MANY GOOD THINGS.

Martha was constantly doing repairs in her mom's house. Helen sent money for the newspaper, insurance, and grass cutting, but she was adamant about not spending money on the old house. She said, "I'll give you money for anything you or Mom need, but I'm not spending one cent on that old house. As far as I'm concerned, it's yours. I don't want any part of it."

One day at work, Martha mentioned to co-workers that her sister sent them money for grass. The looks she received caused her to laugh and say, "Grass *cutting*. You know, lawn mowing." Then they made sport of her for being so naive. Green yard grass was the only kind she thought of.

Since Josephine wasn't writing letters anymore, Martha asked her if she wanted to write to her sister, Lois. She did, so Martha brought paper and pen, and helped with the date, the salutation, and hope you are fine. Then Martha prompted her with questions: Do you want to tell her we did this, and tell her we went there?

So Josephine was able to write a pretty good letter to her sister. Martha told her the address for the envelope, then put a stamp on and mailed it. Lois had no idea that Josephine had not written this entirely by herself and she responded with this letter in return:

Dear Sister,

You and I must be closer than we think because I have been over anxious to find out how you were. I was more excited to get your letter because I have been calling you three and four times a day since last Saturday. I've been letting the phone ring ten times in case you were on the porch.

I tried calling Martha but was told her number was no longer listed. I even tried calling Helen and I only got the answering service and she did not call me back. I was praying to get some kind of sign to know you were alright. Then, here on Monday, here was the little letter in the mail from you. I wouldn't take a thousand dollars for it. I was so relieved to know you were alright. I still call you every morning, but you don't answer. Take good care of yourself. I love you so very much.

The family is all fine but busy with their own life. Garry had spaded the ground around the fence so I still go out every morning to see how the little plants are. I still love my little garden but hate to go out when it gets hot. Lots of love, your sister Lois

Martha had moved her trailer to Port Allen to be closer to work and to have clean water, so her phone number had changed. Helen did not have an answering service so Lois must have dialed the wrong number. And Josephine either wasn't hearing the phone or she was just avoiding it. She knew her limitations. Even with Martha or Helen, she would just unexpectedly hang up the phone. This really hurt people's feelings, especially Helen's. Martha made sure that her aunt had her new phone number after that, and she did have an answer machine to catch calls when she was out. She also helped Josephine call Lois so they could talk.

That fall, Josephine was able to pick some pecans that fell over the fence into her yard. She loved the outdoors, and still could do old familiar things she used to do like gardening.

Martha enrolled her in the Council on Aging Lunch Program. Every weekday a meal was brought to Josephine. She looked forward to them coming by and enjoyed the food. Sometimes she brought it inside and put it on the table and forgot to eat it. Martha now was going over every day after work to check on her.

The Lion's Club loaned them a walker, but Josephine did not like to use it. She could still keep her balance even though she was so bent over, and had difficulty using it correctly. No matter how hard Martha tried, she could not get Josephine to stand near the walker and support her weight on it. Instead, she bent over with her arms extended to grasp the walker. This position gave no support and hurt her back even more.

One day Martha arrived from work to see her mother crying. "Mom, what's wrong?"

"Sally has breast cancer."

Josephine rarely cried, at least in front of others, so this had really upset her. She had grown to love and depend on Sally who lived across the street. Martha was full of Christian do-good-ism, and went to visit Sally. The doctors had determined to give her radium but not chemotherapy, and no operation. This did not seem right, but again, no one questioned the doctor's decision. Maybe it already was too far gone....

Sally continued to get worse, in fact, the cancer soon was a thick, unyielding, solid, and cold mass that seemed so foreign and inappropriate on this woman's chest and reaching into her shoulder. It was not easy to visit and see her grow worse, because Martha was praying aloud for her complete miraculous healing. And she couldn't discontinue the visits because Sally kept asking her to go back. When she did die, though, Sally's family sent Martha a card of thanks writing that Sally said when Martha prayed the pain went away, and they thanked her for being there for Sally. Josephine took her sickness and death as hard as if it had been her daughter, not a neighbor.

Josephine had always had Martha's name on her savings account, and this made it easier to do her banking and pay her bills. Martha was sure to tell Josephine everything that was going on. Josephine trusted her. Martha knew she would have to do all her mother's banking soon, so she took Josephine to the bank to add her name on the C.D. Josephine had bought with the insurance money from the wreck.

The next day Josephine told her neighbor, Mrs. Futrell. That afternoon, when Martha came over to see her, Josephine was very angry with Martha and accused her of stealing from her. When she asked what she meant, Josephine said, "You stole my C.D."

"Mom, no, I didn't, I just got my name put on it so you won't need to go to the bank to handle it. I will have authority to renew it for you. The C.D. is still in the bank in your name and my name. If you want to go talk to them about it and see it's still there, we can go."

"No, it's okay."

Martha was still desperately trying to find the right solution for Josephine's care. She did not want to go to a nursing home. Ty used to say he'd rather die than be put in one and stories on TV told of death and abuse in some, so Josephine would say, "They'll kill you in those places." And Martha felt she really needed to stay in the house where she was familiar, the only home she ever owned.

Martha attended a full Gospel church in Port Allen for a couple of years, but they did not have a Sunday night service so Martha went to Jimmy Swaggart's Family Worship Center on those nights. She also visited other churches and other women's meetings. One of the churches, a large church in a small city nearby, held home groups. Martha still cried a lot and the ladies there tried to help her and always invited her for the "cell" groups. At first these meetings were led by a woman who sought God for the meetings and let the Holy Spirit lead. Men also attended the group. One time a lady from the group had gone to Florida where God was supposedly moving and hurried back to "impart" what she had received to the group by laying hands on them and praying. Strange as it seemed to Martha, she felt oppression instead of relief in most of these meetings. The ladies then tried to cast out spirits of family curses.

It wasn't long before the cell groups changed. The men started going outside the house, and every group was given the same script by the church as to exactly how the meeting was to go. Martha felt they were pushing the Holy Spirit out. The ladies still wanted to help Martha and kept inviting her to the group. Then the church leadership dictated that anyone who would not join their church could not attend the cell group. The ladies apologetically told her this. Martha had attended their church for a few months but quit going, so she told the ladies, "I know you love me and want to help, but I know this is God separating me from you, so I won't attend any more cell meetings." After this the ladies withdrew from Martha even when casually meeting somewhere. It was like; if you're not with us you're against us.

Martha had quit going to the full gospel church and decided to just go to Family Worship center, thinking, "Jimmy Swaggart cries, and if I need to sit in the back of the church and cry through the service, no one will think anything is wrong."

Martha felt a sense of unworthiness, even knowing the scriptures, and all her life she had tried self-helps to make herself better. She often cried during singing and worship and Jimmy Swaggart kept singing and often the mood lifted.

Soon, God began revealing to Brother Swaggart what He had shown the Apostle Paul in Romans chapters six, seven and eight—the way to sanctification and change is the same as for salvation and justification. You just have to place your faith in what Jesus did on the cross, not your own efforts. In time, Martha began to receive freedom from the condemnation. She started saying there were only two works we need to do: FIGHT the good fight of faith, and LABOR to enter into Jesus' rest.

Frances Swaggart felt led of the Lord to start a radio program on their Baton Rouge 88.5 FM station called Sonlife Radio. It began with her reading from the bible, then opening up the phone lines to listeners. Martha called and told her of the situation with Josephine and how she was trying to find the right solutions. Frances was very sympathetic and prayed about it, but made it clear she was most concerned about Josephine being home alone all day.

Martha felt the only solution was to move in with Josephine. She started to clean the bedroom that Ty had used. She also packed and disposed of some of her own things. Norma, in the trailer next door to Martha's, said she had a sister who wanted to buy her trailer so it looked like things were settled. Martha would have a much longer drive to get to work on a busy and rough road, but the biggest problem was the smell in Josephine's house from the termites. They were now destroyed and not entering the house but the residual smell could not be removed. The house was very small, but there was a garage for storage. It had a dirt floor and smelled worse than the house. Martha started cleaning it out and Mr. Tim helped. Martha kept most of the tools, and he took some things Martha didn't want and disposed of the rest.

Helen and Martha's friends did not think it was a good idea for her to move in with her mother, but Martha was grasping for straws.

Josephine's 80th birthday was coming up on Christmas Eve, and Martha wanted her to have a party. Josephine had never had a birthday party, and everyone should celebrate their 80th. So Martha sent out invitations, ordered a cake from the supermarket, made a chocolate cake, and bought soft drinks and snacks. Helen came, as well as twenty other guests. It was a great party and although it was specified no gifts, of course she got lots of great stuff. She and Martha were both touched by the love. The special order cake was awful, but the chocolate cake was good. Josephine still wore her kerchief both inside and outside the house.

Josephine wearing hat and gifts, with Bonnie

Helen's step-kids and Helen gave Josephine earrings, a beautiful scarf, and a big brimmed black hat. She beamed with pleasure, and several pictures were taken of her wearing them. The scarf was draped around her neck and over her shoulder.

Martha moved her bed and a chest of drawers to Josephine's house, but she was really dragging her heels about moving in. She spent most nights there, but the trains about a block away across an open field came through several times a night with their long wailing toots at each crossing, and there were many. Whenever Martha found it unbearable, she made an excuse to go back to her trailer for a night. Since Helen had come for the birthday and Christmas holidays, the girls slept at Martha's trailer.

Norma's sister wanted to buy Martha's trailer, but (Y2K), January 1, 2000 was coming up and she was hesitant to get the loan. The loan company probably was anxious also; as everyone thought the whole system of computers would go down with Y2K, so they were all delaying the sale until after New Year's.

Martha and Helen fixed Christmas dinner, gave their mother her presents, and after she had happily opened them and thanked the girls, they sat down to eat. Martha as usual said Grace, "Dear Heavenly Father, I thank you for this meal and for my mother and sister and that we can be together on Christmas Day, when we celebrate the birth of Jesus. Your word says you'll never put more on us than we can handle, but Lord we've got way more stuff than we can handle."

Martha mostly meant trying to find place for all her clothes and other things in the small house, and knowing that she would be going to work with clothes that smelled bad because of the odorous house. She had already taken her wool coat and better clothes to Helen's house to store.

Helen said, "Martha, I know you want to do the right thing, but I think you're doing the wrong thing by moving in here and so do your friends. You need to move Mom into your trailer. That way you'll both be more comfortable."

Miraculously Josephine agreed. So they had their Christmas dinner then the girls packed up some of Josephine's things and took her to Martha's trailer. Martha made sure that Josephine never entered her house again. It took several months to sell Josephine's house, and when they did go to Plaquemine, and Martha drove past the house to look at it, she asked Josephine if she missed her house and wished she still lived there. She answered, "No, indeed."

Bonnie, one of Helen's step-daughters who worked near Josephine's house visited often, and she visited Martha, also. She called Helen "Mama", and Helen called her daughter. Sometimes when Bonnie had an extra long shift and had to be back on the job in just three or four hours, she stayed at Martha's. Bonnie lived extremely far from her job, so it was good all around that she could bunk with Martha.

Bonnie was such a blessing in helping Martha clean Josephine's house to sell, and she and her husband also built a deck on Martha's trailer with rails so Josephine would be able to sit outside, but still be protected and in the shade. Josephine could also see people as they walked or drove through the park.

Bonnie and her husband Joel building deck

Mrs. Futrell moved away to the other side of town into a larger house and would not have been there any longer for Josephine. Martha thought about how God had provided friends and helpers when they needed them most, and took them away when they no longer needed them.

Mr. Tim kept the yard up until the house sold. Martha gave him enough money to do it for months and he was faithful to mow and trim the yard.

Because of the prior termite infestation, the house did not bring much. The land alone was worth the selling price. Martha probably could have done better, but they had signed with a Realtor, and one deal was flubbed. When the contract was about to expire, they came up with a low offer. Months had gone by and Martha was ready to end this, so they sold. True to her word, Helen wanted no part of the house, and signed her interest over to Martha. The lawyer told her, "You've got a good sister."

"Yes, I have," answered Martha.

Martha enrolled Josephine in the Council on Aging Meals on Wheels Program in Port Allen. Josephine liked the lady who regularly delivered her meals to the trailer.

Norma, in the trailer next door, had two little girls who were of school age. Josephine liked the little girls, but was not very fond of Norma, "That woman is nosy."

"Why do you say that, Mama?"

"Because I always see her looking through her window at me."

Norma proved to be a Godsend to them. She truly worried about Josephine and watched out for her. When she brought Josephine gifts of food, Josephine warmed up to her fast. Norma saw how long Josephine stayed on the porch and watched that she didn't leave while Martha was at work. Josephine never did. She may have forgotten a lot, but she never had left her own house, unless she was going to a neighbor for a specific purpose, and she knew she was home here.

When Helen visited, she took Josephine to the Council on Aging where they could have a meal with others and play bingo. They only allowed Josephine to go with someone who could watch out for her there, and make sure she went to the bathroom. Josephine had been wearing liners to catch any dribbling, and she could hold her urine a long time if necessary, but rules were rules.

Josephine had the largest bedroom with her chiffarobe in it, the one she got for $17.95 when she first got married. The bathroom was between the bedrooms. The central air and heat worked great, and Josephine was not shown how to operate the thermostat this time. Since she didn't like it too cold, Martha used her little window unit in her own room when she slept. Just turning it on briefly made the humidity less in her little room and cooled it down so she could sleep without freezing out Josephine.

To comfort Josephine at night and help her go to sleep, Martha played some music on the tape player. It shut itself off when one side finished so she could just go to sleep without having to bother with turning it off. Martha always asked Josephine if she wanted to hear some music after she went to bed, and nearly always she said yes. The one she played most often was *It Matters To Him About You,* by Jimmy Swaggart. It was slow, soft, and very meaningful to Martha and Josephine during these trying times. It told that God cared about whatever you were going through and loves you; just keep trusting Him.

One day Sister Swaggart played her husband's song, *It Matters to Him About You* at the start of her program. Martha called and told Frances of the changes made for Josephine and that it was the song that she played for Josephine every night before she went to sleep and it comforted both Josephine and Martha. Whether it was coincidence or not, from then on it was played at the start of Frances' program.

Martha had two good friends who visited and they both thought Josephine was so sweet. One of them was an old schoolmate, and Josephine remembered her. Odell was very energetic, outgoing, and optimistic. She called Josephine Mama. Odell didn't drive, so many times Martha, Josephine and Odell went places together.

The other friend was Letty, with whom Martha used to work when she worked for Kathy. They became even closer friends after Martha changed jobs. Letty was a striking lady, much younger than Martha, and Martha always wondered how such a great person wanted to be her friend. Letty was so helpful to Martha in many ways. She had helped Martha when she got behind in her typing and was really edifying in Martha's plight to help her mother. They really were a mutual admiration society. Letty's parents also became friends with Josephine and Martha.

Out for hamburgers one day, Martha had seated Josephine then went to the counter to order. When she returned with the food, she saw a man about Josephine's age stop by the table to say hello to Josephine, who returned the greeting with, "Hello, Tiger." He had a cap on his head with the Louisiana State University Tigers on it.

He, Josephine, and Martha talked at length. He said he had been attending all the LSU games with his family for years, and was on his way to Tiger Stadium for the game. He asked Josephine if Martha was her daughter and she said, "She's my baby." He enjoyed talking with them and had no inkling that Josephine had Alzheimer's.

Martha called her sister and gleefully told her that she had come back to the table to hear her mother flirt with a man, saying, "Hello, Tiger." Then she told Helen the real story.

Josephine and Martha still had many problems needing solutions. Co-workers were a great source of answers. One of them was Millicent, an extremely intelligent lady who knew all the local agencies which were sources of help for senior citizens.

Helen was not able to visit more than four or five times a year, but when she came she stayed about ten days and worked really hard doing the cooking, laundry, and cleaning, and she helped so much with suggestions. She still made sure that Martha took Josephine to the doctor for check-ups and got check-ups for herself.

Martha made pecan pralines for Josephine, who still loved sweets but was real disciplined in that she just ate one every once in a while. The pralines kept well when wrapped individually in cling wrap and put in the refrigerator crisper. There were usually some whenever Helen visited and she thought Martha made them especially for her. Martha would have made them for her anytime so she just let her think they were made for her. Sometimes she did make some to mail to Helen now that she knew she liked them. Helen didn't want many gifts, but when someone surprised her with something it was more meaningful.

Josephine loved red carnations. Martha bought some from the grocery store in mixed flower bouquets occasionally since her mother lived with her, and every time Helen visited. Martha had always wanted flowers but never bought them for herself, and she liked an excuse to get some.

One day Martha came home from work, opened the door and Josephine was not in the kitchen or living room. Fear gripped her. Did Josephine finally wander off looking for her home?

"Mama, Mama," she called, walking down the hall. She found Josephine sitting on the commode.

"Oh, Mom, there you are. Are you okay?"

"Yeah, I'm fine."

Josephine remained there so long that Martha went back and questioned her again, "Mama, how long have you been sitting there?"

"Not long."

"Do you need help?"

"No, I'm going to get up."

Still she did not get up. Martha went back again.

"I'm going to get up."

Finally, Martha realized she was not able to push herself up and there was nothing to hold on to so she could pull up. She said, "Put your hands around my neck, and I'll pull you up."

Josephine could not say how long she was there and was very frightened to be found out. She did not want to admit that she couldn't get up. She seemed so calm that it took Martha a long time to see that Josephine needed help.

"Mama, don't worry, there has to be an answer and we'll figure it out."

Martha told her co-worker Millicent who said the Council on Aging would loan them a potty chair. Martha went to see them and sure enough, there was one that sat over the commode, with a comfortable commode seat, arm rests and adjustable height. Martha took it out of the car and sprayed it down with disinfectant cleaner in the driveway and scrubbed it clean, hosed it off, dried it and set it up over the commode.

"Mama, come sit on this and see if you can get up."

She did. One problem was solved forever.

At this time Josephine could still sit on Martha's stationary bike and pedal, but she wasn't used to it. Once in a while her foot slipped off the pedal, but she was trying to keep moving. Martha put Josephine's glider on the deck, and placed a rocking chair by the front window facing the road through the trailer park, so Josephine could see people come and go. Many waved at her. Josephine liked the friendly people. Martha felt that the movement of gliding and rocking would help exercise muscles and especially internal organs.

Always, whenever Martha was sweeping and asked Josephine to lift her legs so she could sweep she'd say, "Don't sweep under me."

"Why, Mom, you want to get married again?"

"No, indeed."

"Well, that's what they say will happen if someone sweeps under you, that you won't get married again."

"Well, I don't want to get married again."

Martha would go through this same scenario every time, because Josephine forgot and it brought levity between them. Heaven knows, they needed levity.

When Martha got in from work one day, she found the hall carpet near the bathroom soaking wet. Water had reached Josephine's bedroom, also. "Mom, why is the floor wet here? It's soaked."

"I don't know; it must have rained."

"No, Mom, it didn't rain." It took a while to detect what happened. Apparently, Josephine had washed her hands in the lavatory and had not shut the faucet off completely. She always kept the plug in the drain from years of conserving water.

When she realized the lavatory was running over, she shut the water off, pulled the plug, then got a towel and sopped up all the water from the bathroom tile, but couldn't do anything about the carpet. Martha guessed that by the time she came in from work, Josephine had forgotten the episode.

Martha mentally gave her mom at-a-boys for handling the situation as she had. What helped Martha determine what happened was: the floor was wet under the bathroom scale, and when she opened the cabinet under the lavatory, there was a drip down the door.

It took several days of pulling up corners of the carpet, pressing water out of the pad and carpet with towels, and blow drying with her hair dryer before Martha was able to completely dry the plywood floor, pad and carpet.

Oh, yes, she felt very sorry for herself, and complained to everyone who would listen.

Martha tried to give Josephine something to occupy her hands and mind. She could still do many of the things she used to do, like hand sew, peel vegetables and pecans, fold plastic grocery bags, and fold clothes. She appreciated having something to do that made her feel useful.

Martha bought two pieces of material, one with a pink print, and the same pattern in blue. She cut pieces of both colors in eight inch squares and pinned them together with safety pins for Josephine to sew together by hand. She alternated pink and blue, and staggered the colors on the next row so a pink was always next to a blue. It made a checkerboard pattern. Josephine could still thread a needle without glasses and could sew this without supervision. Martha gave her a few squares at a time to sew until it measured about 36X45. Then Martha found a piece of quilting in a complementary color for the backing and sewed it to the checkerboard with the sewing machine. So Josephine made her own afghan to cover her legs when her knees got cold and ached from the arthritis.

This kept Josephine so busy and happy that Martha thought, what else can she sew? She got more cloth and cut out an apron, ironed and pinned the edges so Josephine could stitch a hem around it, and cut, ironed and pinned the sashes. When Josephine did the sashes, Martha sewed them to the apron. She used grip fasteners on the neck strap so it did not have to be pulled over the head. Then they made a few more aprons.

Josephine beams over the winning ribbons

Martha told Millicent at work about the aprons her mom made. Millicent said, "You should enter them in the County Fair."

Martha got the details and took her mom to enter two aprons. They walked from the car into the pavilion where they would be displayed, and the aprons were entered in two separate categories; Clothing, apron, and Clothing, any other garment. Josephine won $3.00 for each apron and two third place ribbons.

Millicent also told Martha that she had a sister-in-law who sat with the elderly, and that she was very reliable and sweet. Molly was the sister of Millicent's husband. Martha said, "If she's as sweet as you are, she's very sweet." Millicent said, "Molly is sweeter."

Martha was very reluctant to have a stranger come in to sit in their home, but since she knew Millicent so well she arranged to have Molly come visit. Martha asked Molly to come as a visitor who could be a friend, not as a sitter. This worked out so well that Josephine loved Molly and always thought that she was only her friend and never learned Martha paid her. Molly reciprocated with love in return and she and Josephine enjoyed conversing in French or just spending quiet time together.

When Molly sat with Josephine, Martha could shop or just have time for herself. Martha always had something cooked, and Molly served it and cleaned up afterward. This was about the extent of Molly's duties. When Josephine later grew incontinent and soaked through her adult diapers, Josephine never realized she had, and Molly never intruded on her privacy. Martha made a protective cushion for the rocker recliner she surrendered to her mother to prevent it from getting wet or smelly.

14

Josephine's Best Year

Josephine remembered less of recent events, and thought more on events of bygone days. She often told Martha how Garry caused Jill to hit her. Martha told her that she needed to forgive them; the Bible says you have to forgive so God can forgive you. She never wanted to forgive, although she loved her brother and sister and had never shown any animosity toward them. It was just childhood memories that came up to her like they were recent.

That winter Martha took Josephine to see a pageant at a Baptist Church in Baton Rouge. It was called Twin Living Christmas Trees and it was a spectacular presentation with people positioned to form the "trees" while singing carols. There were wooden soldiers, bears, many characters, and the story of redemption. It was rather long and by the time they gave the invitation for salvation, Josephine was ready to go. They had provided a wheelchair so Martha could push Josephine to their seats and back to the car.

Martha did not want to get Josephine her own wheelchair because she wanted her to continue walking as long as she could. When her knee got too bad, Martha took her to the Orthopedist who injected cortisone which helped for about a year.

Martha always feared that she would not be able to care for her mother if she became bedridden. Josephine had taken care of Richard, but Martha knew she would not be strong enough, physically or mentally, to do it.

Josephine had not been in a bathtub in a long time and she did not want a shower spraying on her head, so they continued to wash her with a washcloth she dipped in the lavatory. Josephine got the parts she could reach, and Martha got her back and gave her pedicures. Martha had been giving her pedicures for a couple of years now, since she and Helen had bought Josephine a new pair of shoes for Mother's Day and wanted her to try them on. When removing her old shoes, they discovered the socks stuck to her toes with a yellow gunk. Upon removing the socks they could see the toenails had piled up over themselves since the socks had not been removed in a long time. Josephine's Alzheimer's caused her to forget to wash her feet or cut her toenails. Regular pedicures brought the toenails back to normal.

The first time that Martha gave her a manicure and polished her fingernails a light pink, Josephine was so proud. "Mom, let's take a picture," Martha said as she got her camera. Josephine was beaming as she placed her hands across each other on her chest displaying the pretty pink fingernails. She had bitten her fingernails all her life, but now she did not.

Norma from next door continued to visit Josephine and bring her goodies. Norma's sister had been disappointed that after Y2K, instead of being able to buy the mobile home, Martha and Josephine kept it, since Martha had not moved into her mother's house. She kept asking Martha when they would buy a house so she could have the mobile home.

Martha had been on the lookout to buy a house ever since she moved back to Louisiana. First, she was afraid she couldn't afford it, but more than that, she knew she could not move far away from her mother. Twice she did seriously go to look at houses, and each time her car overheated so she gave it up. It was like a sign from God. She asked, "God, when will I ever be able to buy a house?"

Now they had sold Josephine's house, with Martha getting half interest in it since Helen had given her fourth to her, and she had a buyer for her trailer. The big holdup now was finding a house in the area she wanted near Family Worship Center. Mrs. Frances Swaggart had expanded her radio program and invited guests to join her in person or by phone. They covered various interesting topics and soon had a large listening audience. She now called it Frances and Friends. She had listeners from all over the country over the network of radio stations and the internet.

Finally one day Martha saw a For Sale sign on a house near the church. A man and his son were having a garage sale in the driveway and carport. She stopped and asked, "Have you sold my house yet?" She should not have asked that, because she wound up paying way more than she should have. The two men smoked and had a cat. It took two years to really get the smell and cat hairs out. Martha hired two women to go in and clean the house. It smelled better initially, but that was because of so much bleach. The ladies did a once-over of the appliances, bathroom and floors, but this house needed a scrubbing all over, even the walls, and the refrigerator needed a detailed cleaning.

Martha had been packing some things, and had a lot of Josephine's things still boxed, so they began moving when the purchase became final. Martha got a moving company to move them. The charge was $300 and $100 more for an extra hour. Martha and one good man could have done it in two hours, but these guys were undoubtedly told to dawdle. And dawdle they did! When Martha started removing things from the freezer to pack in an icebox, they said, don't do that yet! That should have given her a clue. The next clue was when they did not want to back the truck near the door, but left it on the street. The third was when they did not use a dolly, but insisted on carrying everything one at a time.

Martha started carrying things out herself, but they could not be hurried. Of course, in the end, she had to pay more for the extra time. The men did set up the furniture and Martha made the beds. She had to tack a sheet in the window of Josephine's bedroom because it was bare. All the blinds had to be removed for cleaning and more had to be purchased.

Norma was an angel and made a casserole of chicken and cheesy noodles so they would have something to eat until they could unpack. She said, "You have to come back and visit me so you can bring the dish back then." Her sister was ready to buy the trailer, so they had to come back to complete the sale anyway.

The casserole was delicious; they used paper plates and heated the food in the microwave. They were so thankful to wonderful Norma. Josephine had become very fond of Norma and was sad to say goodbye, but they kept in touch awhile.

The next day Martha and Josephine went out for breakfast to celebrate their first day in their new home. They were happy. But when Martha got a good look at the house in the light of day, she was not so happy with it. It was very dirty and needed extensive repair and remodeling.

When she saw Sister Swaggart she told her of purchasing the house and its condition, and that she regretted buying it. Frances put it in perspective for her. She basically told Martha she should be thankful;

didn't she think it was better to own than rent? Martha saw the wisdom in that and worked hard to clean and repair the house.

When Martha dropped Josephine off in front of Family Worship Center, helped her out of the car and up the steps, a church greeter and long-time friend of Martha's, Dorothy Ellis, met Josephine to help her in. Josephine loved the attention. This went on for weeks. One day, Dorothy and her daughter both went to hug her, and chuckled when Josephine said, "Don't y'all fight over me."

Now that Martha was grooming Josephine, and reminding her to put lip balm on her lips frequently, she didn't get sores or split lips anymore. By now the hairdresser who cut their hair had graduated medical school and had quit hairdressing. Martha began cutting Josephine's hair. It was a lovely shiny gray with only a few black strands. Martha was able to fix it attractively, but Josephine still wanted to wear her kerchief all the time. Martha asked, "Mom, when you die, do you want to be in the coffin with your kerchief?"

"No, I want to look pretty. I won't be cold then."

It wouldn't be long until Josephine did not wear a kerchief all the time. Maybe she wasn't as cold in the new house, and the car was heated beforehand, or maybe she just forgot.

Sometimes Josephine had trouble getting out of the recliner, and Martha heard her tell herself, "Get up, Josie."

Helen sent money so Martha would get a special recliner for Josephine, but Josephine preferred the one she had been using. Martha did not find the new recliner comfortable either.

The Realtor who sold Josephine's house kept in touch and after hearing they bought a new house she wrote to Martha that she was happy to know everything was going so well and her mother was content.

Molly continued to sit with Josephine at least once a week. Molly did not charge much compared to most sitters, so Martha paid her one dollar more an hour since she had to drive farther. Josephine still thought of her as a good friend, and never questioned whether she got paid to be with her. She did know that Molly sat with others and asked, "You get paid for that, right?"

Martha began repairs to the house and found a handy man who did not charge much. He was partial to Martha because she was caring for her mother. He installed a long shower hose with an on-off lever at the end near the shower head so that the water could be shut off or on without turning the faucets while showering. This came in handy for giving Josephine a shower without wetting her head.

Josephine and Martha had a lot of laughs together. Martha had to watch her take her vitamins because she had two or three in her mouth at a time trying to swallow them. Now Martha made her open her mouth and stick out her tongue to prove she had swallowed it before she could take the next one. Martha opened her mouth and stuck out her tongue, so Josephine would do it right back, and they'd laugh about it wondering what other people would think of two old women sticking their tongues out at each other.

Sometimes, as in the case of the calcium tablet, it would start dissolving so the coating would be gone. The pill was too rough to swallow, so Martha made her take it out of her mouth and throw it away. Josephine really tried to swallow it because she hated to waste anything.

Whenever Josephine tasted something she liked, she closed her eyes, opened them, smiled, and said, "Good." Josephine liked Martha's cooking. They had similar tastes.

Someone from Jimmy Swaggart's church told Martha about a great adult daycare facility only a quarter mile from their house. Martha thought Josephine would not get in trouble but knew it still was not good for her to spend all day alone while she was at work. The neighbors here did not know them and would not know to watch out for her.

Martha called and got information about the daycare and just dropped in one afternoon after work to check it out. It happened that people were picking up their family members to take them home, so Martha was able to sit and watch unobserved for a few minutes before she was noticed. She then said she was interested in daycare for her mother, and they were invited to an open house. It was near Christmas time.

Martha took Josephine, got her seated, and went to get her mom some refreshments. One of the ladies that cared for the people, named Tammy, saw that Josephine's nose was dripping from an allergy so she took a tissue and wiped Josephine's nose. Martha knew that Josephine would be cared for here. All the caretakers were black, and so was the nurse. Tammy became Martha's favorite although all the workers were terrific.

There was a process of filling out forms, having a social worker visit their home, and getting a physical exam before Josephine would be accepted. The social worker told them that there were Medicaid spots for people without resources, and Martha should look into qualifying for that. Martha knew that the money her mother had so painstakingly saved all these years, though not much, would be a hindrance. She got her mother enrolled in daycare as a paying client, and took her to Social Security to see if she could get on Medicaid. They were asked about assets, and Martha produced records. The lady asked how much of this was Josephine's, and if she owed anyone anything. Martha said that she had paid a lot of necessities from her own money, but how do you charge your own mother for anything? The lady was really trying to get Martha to say if Josephine owed her money, but Martha didn't want to tell of her own money that she had spent, especially in front of her mother. She didn't want her mom to feel bad and it just didn't seem right to charge your mother for care.

It was determined that the amount of money Josephine had in the bank needed to be spent down, and accounting for portions of rent, utilities and Josephine's daycare, plus medicine, clothing, other necessities, that it would take a few months to do so. They continued to pay for daycare, and got on the list for Medicaid. One day the letter came that she was now eligible. Not long after, an opening for a Medicaid slot at daycare became open.

Martha made a cloth bag to fasten to the handlebars of the walker. The straps were attached with grip fasteners, and the bag was closed with a button down flap. Josephine was able to keep her lipstick, lip balm, tissues, and eyeglasses handy without having to hold on to them.

It was a Catholic daycare, and besides keeping them up to date on the news, the day of the week and the date, they also recited the rosary for those who wanted to join in, so Josephine brought hers. Martha was a Born Again Christian and no longer believed in the Catholic Church. Although Josephine prayed to receive salvation every time they prayed the sinner's prayer in church for new converts, and believed the new truths she learned, she still reverted to the childhood beliefs of the Catholic Church. She said she'd be a Catholic until she died and recited the rosary with the others.

The ladies kept the clients active, playing bingo and cards, music and singing, chair exercises, and saw to it they went to the bathroom on time. A change of clothes was kept for each person, so Martha marked Josephine's clothes *Josie* for short. Later Martha could not remember if Josephine had told herself, "Get up, Josie" before or after Josephine went to daycare. She also wrote *Josie* on her catch-all bag and rosary. A couple of years after Josephine no longer attended daycare, the rosary was returned to Martha, having been found in the possession of another daycare client. The ladies all called Josephine Ms. Josie.

Everyone at daycare was treated with respect. Whenever a client told a story about the past, it was accepted as very interesting. As the Director said, "Here it's a win-win situation for the clients. They are always treated like they are okay, and whatever they say is not questioned."

Josephine absolutely blossomed. She loved daycare and would gladly get out of bed to be bathed and dressed to go. They fed a mid-morning snack, lunch, and a mid-afternoon snack at daycare. Martha didn't realize how much they were fed and made sure Josephine had a good breakfast and vitamins every morning. Josephine gained a little weight.

At night and weekends Martha worked on the house, remodeling one room at a time. She left the TV on a good program for Josephine and worked in another room. Whenever she walked back into the room where her mother sat, she saw relief on Josephine's face. She forgot that Martha told her she would be working in another room.

There was wallpaper to strip, sheetrock patches to do, plaster to fill in, walls to paint, and bathrooms to remodel. The carpet was badly stained and smelled. It could not be cleaned even though a professional was hired, so Martha stripped out the carpet, and when all the rooms were painted and completed, she had new carpet installed.

There was an extra room where Martha was able to hang clothes she rinsed out when Josephine had an "accident." Helen sent some cotton covered rubber sheets and pads. Martha put them over the mattress then put a regular mattress pad and sheet, then a small flannel lined rubber pad over the center area. At first only the pad got wet, but as time went by, Josephine could not be budged to get up at night to be changed. Martha was counseled to just wait until morning, since she was missing sleep and Josephine did not want to get up, so everything was very wet in the morning.

Martha had gone for counseling several times with Reverend Dave Smith who was, and is at this writing on the pastoral staff of Family Worship Center, and a teacher and principal of Family Christian Academy and has been a part time professor at WEBC, (World

Evangelism Bible College). Brother Dave had helped Martha sort out her feelings and options regarding her self and motives in her choices by carefully phrased questions. He also advised that letting Josephine sleep all night was better for her and Martha than trying unsuccessfully to rouse her and get her to the bathroom.

At church one Sunday, before the service started, Josephine wet her pants a bit in the bathroom. Martha didn't want her embarrassed and asked her if she could walk to the car. Josephine said yes so they went out a door near the restroom so no one would see them in the lobby. Josephine did not have her walker and she tired out and fell in the lot at the front of the car. A man was walking by them to go into church and he immediately came and lifted Josephine up off the asphalt and helped her into the car. Martha was so grateful, asking his name. He was Anthony Hawkins, and thereafter, every time Martha saw him, she went to greet him and talk to him. They became good friends.

Josephine was easy to wake up in the morning. She slept in her socks and would not walk without her shoes, so Martha put them on her while she sat on the edge of the bed, then helped her up, giving her the walker. Martha took her to sit on the commode first thing, giving her orange juice to drink. Josephine believed that the juice helped her to use the bathroom. Meanwhile Martha prepared the table with everything needed for breakfast, then returned to Josephine.

With the six foot shower hose and a bathtub seat Martha could shower Josephine. It was a test of faith on Josephine's part as Martha helped Josephine undress, except for her shoes and then had her back up to the tub, hold Martha around the neck while Martha held her under the arms to lower her to the seat. In this manner, Josephine had to sit down on the bench by faith; she couldn't see it or touch it until she sat. This method never failed, and though Josephine fell a couple of times in other circumstances, she never had an accident in the tub.

Then Martha removed her shoes and socks and helped her turn and put her feet in the tub. Josephine lathered herself where she could reach and Martha did her back, legs and feet, then rinsed her with the hose. The shower felt so good to Josephine, with warm water running all over her body.

The process was reversed to get out. Her body was dried somewhat, her legs and feet dried well, lotion and powder applied and Martha helped her turn again to get her legs over the edge of the tub while Josephine remained seated. Martha put her socks and shoes on her feet and helped her up with the same grip they had before. Then she was thoroughly dried, (deodorant, lotion and powder applied), dressed, and taken to the table for breakfast.

While Josephine ate, Martha in her own bathroom cried, prayed, showered, and dressed, then watched her mother take her vitamins. Then it was off to day care and to work. Martha felt so stretched and stressed and was really frightened thinking that her mother could outlive her. She felt her own life would not improve if her mother was gone, in fact, she would feel more lonely and without purpose. But fear of the future was a near reality. It was getting harder.

At daycare a problem arose. When Martha went to pick up Josephine, the caregivers told her that Ms. Josie did not want to go to the bathroom for them anymore, saying, "I didn't drink anything, and I don't need to go."

Martha said, "We've worked out problems before, and we'll figure this out, too."

At home, Martha made a small card and typed on it, "Mom, daycare rules say you have to go to the bathroom every two hours, so when the ladies ask you to go, just go with them." She punched two holes in the top, folded it in two, and threaded it on a pretty black cord. She also attached a silver ornament to it, making it like a necklace. Josephine liked necklaces, especially the cheap Mardi Gras necklaces that her sister and nieces had given her in bundles from 'way down the bayou. Martha gave the note necklace to Josephine and asked her to read it. Josephine looked at it and said, "But I don't need to go."

Martha grabbed it back and added, "whether you need to go or not." The ladies at day care were told to ask Josie to read the card necklace when it was time to go and they had no more problems getting her up after that. Josephine could still read and comprehend and she always obeyed rules. So whenever Martha had something she wanted Josephine to remember, she wrote it out for her.

It was farther to visit Josephine's family, and vice versa, but they did visit a lot. Garry's wife started getting Parkinson's disease. He had heart problems, but kept taking care of her. Their two sons were married and also devoted to their mother. Garry grew worse, and when Lois told Martha and Josephine that Garry was in the hospital, they both wanted to go see him. It was a teaching hospital and he was very ill. When Josephine and Martha visited him in the room he appeared to be in a coma. Martha felt no response, nor did she sense that his soul or spirit acknowledged their presence. In Martha's opinion, he had passed on, yet they kept him alive on machines possibly experimenting on him. A week or two later, the family said enough and they removed the machines. The sons continued to care for their mother.

Martha and Josephine went to the funeral service, and Josephine's other brother, T-Brou, was there. He, Martha and Josephine had written to each other a couple of years earlier. Martha made sure she wrote to him about forgiveness and Jesus.

Now T-Brou was also getting dementia, but had driven himself to the funeral. He had a son and a daughter on whom he doted. Martha went to talk to him and told him she was Josephine's daughter and that Josephine was there. "Phene's here? Where? I want to see her."

Martha brought him to where Josephine was sitting and said, "Mom, it's Uncle T-Brou."

Brother and sister were so happy to see each other after all these years. Martha let them sit next to each other during the service. But after awhile, Josephine forgot who he was, and told Martha, "If that man gets any closer to me, I'm going to hit him."

"Mo-om! That's your brother T-Brou!"

"It is? Oh, I didn't know."

He forgot who Josephine was, too.

Back home in Baton Rouge, Martha went to Alzheimer's meetings held in the same building as the day care. So much is still unknown about Alzheimer's. No one attributed it to head injuries, but Martha continued to believe her mother's was caused by the truck accident in 1984, where she hit the left part of her forehead at the hairline against the windshield and metal frame of the roof.

Both the social worker and the leaders of the Alzheimer's meetings talked about quality of life. They made Martha feel very uncomfortable and helpless. She was doing all she could for her mother. She took her to enjoyable places even when she knew that as much as Josephine enjoyed an ice cream cone, after it was gone and the taste was still in her mouth, she forgot she had eaten it. It took weeks before Martha realized they weren't talking about Josephine's quality of life, but Martha's. And there wasn't much she could do to improve that.

Martha had to label things she didn't want Josephine to hide or get into, so she kept medicines in a plastic bag labeled *Martha's Medicine*. Josephine never touched anything that was labeled as someone else's.

Cara met Josephine and all the other clients of the daycare at the door when they drove up. Cara was a volunteer who rose very early in the morning to greet them and get them safely inside. She worked until 11 AM and was very faithful, never missing a day. Evana, the nurse, was very sensitive and caring, and very much by the book as far as health went. Dedra, the director, ran a tight ship, but never was too busy to talk to the clients or their families and make them feel special.

Martha had asked if they had rockers Josephine could use. They said they did, but she found they were in a room that was seldom used, and Josephine and the others sat in large straight chairs. At home Josephine sat in the rocker recliner, so she rocked at home.

Helen continued to fly to Baton Rouge four or five times a year to help out for ten days at a time. She did all the cooking and cleaning, and whatever else she could. Just having her there to share the responsibility was a great relief to Martha. Helen made everything more fun, too. When the horse races were on TV, she involved Josephine and Martha. Helen knew all the horses, the jockeys, trainers and owners. She could often spot a winner. She had a theory that if a horse pooped on the walk to the track, that horse would win.

It never failed. Josephine was very good at picking a winner also. Martha had no clue and just chose one with a catchy name or if the odds were something like five to one. This betting had no money involved.

Helen still liked sausage biscuits and made going out for one a special occasion. She cooked colorful meals and fancy desserts like Creme Brulee.

When Helen and Martha went to pick Josephine up at daycare one afternoon, they saw Josephine and Dedra talking. Josephine was all excited and animated and doing most of the talking, with Dedra listening intently, smiling and agreeing. Helen said. "Look at that. Mom never talks that much to us." When Martha talked to Dedra about it later, Dedra said it was because at daycare, Josephine could not make a mistake and nobody was going to correct her. Josephine felt like a person with valuable experiences at daycare. Martha realized that she often did correct her mother, so Josephine didn't talk as much around her. It made things confusing for Josephine to have what was her reality questioned by her daughter whom she trusted. Dedra also said her mother sang out loud in the sing-alongs and led *When the Saints go Marching In.* When Martha asked her to sing it for her, she was pleasantly flabbergasted to hear her sing it very well.

While lying in bed, Josephine saw the shadows on the blown ceiling at home and thought it was dirty, or thought there was a bug on the ceilings or walls. A leaf in the yard looked like a bird. Martha felt Josephine trusted her because she told the truth as much as possible, but in correcting her mother she was really confusing her. At the Alzheimer's meetings they always said, "Just let them live in whatever world they are in." One lady visited her dad in an Alzheimer's unit of a nursing home and if he said he had been fishing, she just asked him if he caught any. Martha wished she could do that but she never could. She had to say, "No, Mom, that's not a bird, it's a leaf."

After the September eleventh terrorist attack, it became harder to fly. Helen had to put up with delays and heightened security on the flights and also had to coordinate rides to the airports and back. It generally meant riding a bus, walking part of the way, and getting a friend to take her part way. Once in New Orleans, some of her step-kids usually picked her up to take her to Baton Rouge where she spent a night or two with them before she went to Martha's house. There were no direct flights from the airport nearest her house to Baton Rouge.

Every time the TV rebroadcast the film of the 9/11 terrorist attacks and the planes hit the twin towers, Josephine thought it had just happened. She always was horrified anew because she promptly forgot she had already seen it. Since it was such a terrible event the news media replayed it often.

Josephine's arthritis was getting bad in her shoulders, so Martha learned to put her tee shirt on by having her stick her arms through the armholes first in front of her body, then Martha pulled the neck opening over her head and straightened the shirt down around her body. She reversed the procedure to take it off, pulling it up in the back and over her head, then off her arms in front of her. Martha always told the people at daycare all these tips. There were four ladies who did the hands-on caring and there was no turnover, so they could know what worked for each client and were sure to take very good care of them.

Josephine had a lot of friends at daycare. One of them was Jane, who was a new client. Jane and Josephine talked a lot together and got along great. Jane often had peppermints and always gave her some. Anyone who gave her food was extra special. Josephine often told Martha, "Jane might not be pretty but she sure is a good friend."

For Easter, Josephine could still dip the boiled eggs in the dye and turn them into beautiful colored eggs with no mess. She and Martha always got invitations to the big family occasions like Easter with Helen's step kids who treated them like family, too. Martha still loved the big family gatherings.

Josephine had written down her favorite recipes through the years, and she remembered how to cook. Whenever Martha asked Josephine how to cook certain foods, Josephine could still tell her, even though it sometimes it took a little prompting: "Mom, I want to make some sweet potato pies. Can you help me?"

"Sure."

"I've got this can of sweet potatoes; do I drain it and mash the potatoes?"

"Yeah, mash them with sugar and butter."

By asking questions, and Josephine saying or showing her how much of each ingredient to put in, Martha made delicious sweet potato pies just like her mother's.

Here's the recipe:

Josephines Sweet Potato Pies

Mash together:

    1 large can yams, drained

    2/3 cup sugar

2 teaspoons vanilla

2 teaspoons cinnamon

1/4 teaspoon fresh grated nutmeg

3 Tablespoons melted butter

Sift together:

2 cups flour

3/4 teaspoon salt

2 teaspoons baking powder

In separate bowl beat together:

2 eggs

1 teaspoon almond extract

1/3 cup cooking oil

1 teaspoon vanilla

1/3 cup sugar

Add flour mixture to egg mixture alternating with just enough milk to make dough firm enough to handle without being sticky, (no more than 1/3 cup milk). Divide dough into six balls, rolling each out into a circle on well-floured board. Place a large spoonful of the potato mixture on half of the circle, fold dough over the potato and crimp the edges with a fork dipped in flour to seal edges. Momma says to oil the pan first. Bake in preheated 400 degree oven until lightly browned.

Martha could cook anything from casseroles to stews with Josephine's directions. Martha liked cushaws, which were like a pumpkin with a long gooseneck. Martha cut it in slices and she and Josephine peeled them and diced them on cutting boards. Josephine loved to do things she still could handle, like peel and chop vegetables. After they had chopped them, Martha wanted to cook some, so she started boiling some in a pot and sat her mom on a stool near her so she could monitor the progress as Martha cooked.

Josephine was really getting tired, but she wanted to help so she didn't say anything. At one point, Josephine leaned back to make room for Martha and lost her balance. She threw out her arm and brushed Martha as she tried not to fall, but she was behind Martha, and Martha could not catch her. The stool fell down with her. She fell on her rump. X-Rays showed no broken bones, but she did hurt for a couple of weeks. Josephine had fallen a couple of times before, and Martha had to get a neighbor to help her up.

The social worker suggested a memory training course that was available and Josephine was willing to take it. It did improve her memory a little. Whenever Josephine ate right and was happy, with no stress, her memory was much better. By now she was on Alzheimer's prescription medication and the major pain reliever prescription medication for arthritis. Martha found that herbal products really helped her memory, also. When the arthritis made Josephine more bent over than ever, she got physical therapy at daycare. It was pretty strenuous and they continued as long as there was improvement.

There were many activities for them at daycare. Sometimes they went on an outing in the bus or van to ride around sightseeing and stop for ice cream. That was Josephine's favorite thing. Sometimes they had snowballs. Josephine had a really fun time when she could stick out her tongue at Martha and show that her tongue was still blue. Blueberry was her favorite. They also celebrated birthdays and holidays and often had little prizes they could take home.

"Don't sweep under me, Martha."

"What's the matter, Mama, you want to get married again?" Martha continued to tease her mother and make jokes.

"Oh, no, I don't want to get married again."

The social worker had been telling Martha she should put Josephine in a nursing home, because if she needed to go suddenly, it might be difficult to get her in a good one right away. Everyone was more worried about Martha than Josephine. Whenever Martha asked

Josephine that since she liked daycare so much, would she like it if they had a bed and she could stay there all the time, she said, "No, I don't want to stay there to sleep."

During the months following, Martha asked her the same question, and it was always the same, "No, I don't want to stay there to sleep."

At times Josephine would indicate that Martha *should* take care of her since she birthed her, nursed her and cared for her. "Mom, it's much easier to handle a baby and care for them than it is to care for an adult. You know, there's that saying that a mother can take care of twelve children, but twelve children can't take care of one mother."

15

Downhill from Here

It got harder to convince Josephine to go to the bathroom or be changed. She kept saying she didn't need to. Martha couldn't use the "daycare rules" at home.

After Josephine fell, Martha started worrying about how suddenly something can happen and felt that she could not handle caring for Josephine if she couldn't walk. For fifteen years, Lois took care of her mother-in-law who had Alzheimer's and was not pleasant to deal with. Lois had her own children nearby but even so had a hard time caring for her mother-in-law and could sympathize with Martha's plight, even though Josephine had never gotten mean. She was still sweet and everybody loved her. But she was difficult to handle because her mind didn't always show her reality, like when she needed to go to the bathroom.

Martha tried to see about getting funded home care, but very little funds were allocated for home care. Most of it went to nursing homes because of nursing home lobbyists. And Josephine really didn't want anyone else except Martha to do anything for her. They had tried several other sitters who were able and willing to bathe and change her, but Josephine told them no, Martha would do it. The only alternative for them was nursing homes. So Martha asked around and found one which was known as the best in the area and got Josephine on the list. It wasn't more than a month later; she got a call to offer her the slot. Martha said, "Oh, no, we're not ready for a nursing home yet."

Martha got a call to put her mom in the nursing home every month or so. She always refused. Neither she nor Josephine was ready to consider the nursing home. But Josephine's knee started giving her trouble.

It was difficult to walk and Martha worried that someday she would not be able to walk at all.

Molly came to sit with Josephine about once a week even though there was day care. Martha was so relieved that she didn't have to worry about her mom being okay all day while she worked or shopped, and knowing that Josephine was enjoying herself.

Martha was still overwhelmed with so much to do: all the legal, medical, and other issues, plus all the work that needed doing in the house and yard. She wasn't thinking clearly or she might have remembered that cortisone shots had relieved the pain in Josephine's knee.

She really was operating in fear and fatigue, mostly fear. Fear that her mother would not be able to walk, and fear her mother could outlive her. She still had people on all sides telling her how a whole team of people in a nursing home would be able to give her mother better care than she could. No one would blame Martha for putting her in a nursing home, not even Lois. She, above all, understood what it was like. Except for arthritis and Alzheimer's Josephine was in great health, and had always worked hard and eaten right. Martha had done a great job with keeping her healthy and groomed.

But Martha began to buckle under the decision. With the help of her old schoolmate, Odell, she arranged with the Director of Admittance to give her mother a tour of the best nursing home in Baton Rouge which took Medicaid to see if she might like it.

Josephine loved Odell, having known her a long time. Odell joked with her and called her Mama. So they told Josephine they wanted her to see a wonderful place that was just like daycare. Josephine was transported through the place in a wheelchair, and saw prime areas. No matter what they said about it, no matter how good some of it might look, she still knew it was a nursing home.

After they were in the car again, Martha asked Josephine if she would like to stay there. She said in a flat voice, "If I have to."

But the wheels were already in motion. Josephine enjoyed the Holidays, Thanksgiving, her birthday on Christmas Eve, Christmas and New Years at daycare and at home. In February she had a new step-great, great grandchild, a beautiful black haired girl. She held the three day old child cradled in her arms with a look of exquisite joy and wonder on her face.

Then in the spring, the bottom dropped out of her world. Martha didn't have the courage to bring her to the nursing home alone; she got the Social Worker to go with them to admit her. They took her directly from daycare, so daycare became a place of treachery in Josephine's mind.

The administrator who had tried for months to get Martha to put her in the nursing home promised that they would help Josephine walk with her walker, and wheel her in a wheelchair for long distances. It wasn't until after she was admitted that they told Martha that help walking would only be done as therapy by order of the doctor, and Martha knew from the daycare therapy that it was very vigorous, so she didn't get it.

Josephine submitted bravely to entering the nursing home. Martha hoped she wouldn't be that aware of it, but she was. She was given a room, and immediately the head nurse came to give her a physical. It involved a strip search to be sure she did not have any wounds or bruises. Josephine did not want anyone except Martha to see her undressed, but this was a nurse, and she had always complied with doctors and nurses.

Everything was out of Martha's hands now. She tried to get acquainted with the staff to tell them the best way to get Josephine's cooperation, and how to dress her without hurting her. But the staff was too large, and shift changes were frequent. They were too overworked and underpaid to care. When they washed and changed her, they hurt her shoulders, and she would look at Martha and say, "Look how they are hurting me."

Everyone told Martha that she should just stay away for a week and that Josephine would adjust better. They did not know Josephine. Or Martha.

The bad thing was, since Josephine was not confrontational and would not try to escape, they put her in the regular unit, not the Alzheimer's unit. So she appeared to have all her mental faculties.

Josephine was placed in a wheelchair and left to her own devices, except when she had an appointment for the beauty shop, a shower, or meal times. The footrests were removed from the wheelchairs and discarded. It was expected that the clients would use their feet and walk the wheelchair around. Josephine never did that and couldn't learn how, so she stayed where she was placed. If anyone asked her if she needed changing, or to go to the bathroom, Martha never knew it, and of course Josephine did not want to. The first day Martha returned to find her mother soaking wet. She asked why she had not been changed and they said, "If she doesn't want, we don't force her." Some care, being left to her own devices!

Medication was out of Martha's control, also. She did not know that they were giving her medicines for something Josephine didn't have. When she did find out and told their family doctor, he said she never had that.

Martha left her in the dining room for supper the first day. After a couple of hours she returned to see her mother still there. She asked the nurses and they told her she would say she was still eating and just left her there alone, except for the kitchen help who would have liked to finish and go home.

Josephine just didn't want to go to bed. She said people will kill you here. Martha, with the help of an aide, got her to bed, but for a week Josephine would not sleep. She had a roommate behind a curtain, and the woman cried out every once in a while. Doors slammed often as nurses went in and out of the supply cabinet nearby. Josephine was afraid.

Martha called Lois so Josephine could talk to her. Josephine kept thinking that Lois would come get her and rescue her and take her to live with her.

A pitcher of water was put on her nightstand, but she wasn't able to pour it and no one except Martha offered her a drink. To keep her hydrated, Martha requested that at meals they give Josephine a glass of water as well as milk. That helped keep her hydrated. She was still able to eat alone.

She was never taken out of the wheelchair except by Martha, or to put her to bed. The staff had orders not to. Either they didn't have time, (except many times they would watch TV), or they were afraid if she fell and hurt herself they would be sued. She was not changed and sat in her own urine unless Martha got them to wash and change her.

Martha went every day and spent much of the day there. She would find Josephine slumped over with her torso over her knees and her head and arms hanging down. When she'd say, "Mom, you're going to fall out," she'd say no, she liked to sit like that. Martha didn't know if she was despondent or drugged. The director threatened to tie her to the chair, despite Martha telling him not to.

Josephine told Martha that there was a male nurse and she was afraid. She did not want men handling her. In being bathed or changed, she thought everyone just wanted to see her naked. Martha kept trying to make things work out, but it was too much. Josephine was so fearful that she wouldn't allow herself to fall asleep, even with Martha sitting near her bed.

Martha thought she could have a heart attack. After six days, Martha went to church and asked God how she could manage her mother's care if she took her out of the nursing home. She came up with a plan. She went to the nursing home and told Josephine, "Mom, I'm sorry I put you in here, and I am going to try to get you out in the morning and take you home. I'm going to stay with you all night."

She did stay the night but even then Josephine did not sleep. In the morning Martha called the daycare to see if they would be able to take her back. They said if Martha paid the cost of the stay at the nursing home, they could, and they would be glad to have her back. Martha also arranged to take early retirement so she could cope better. So Martha got Josephine discharged and brought her home and put her to bed. Josephine was so tired that she slept for hours, and it was daytime.

Martha called her job and requested a couple of days' annual leave to keep Josephine home to rest. She tried to reassure her that she was living at home again and was going to daycare just like before. But the traumatic experience took its toll on Josephine. Her mind really couldn't deal with what she had been through. She now was angry and distrustful of Martha.

She felt outcast and betrayed at daycare; they knew she had been away, and things weren't the same. At home and at daycare she muttered all the time, about the good Martha and the bad Martha. To her, it was like Martha was two different people, one she could trust, and the other she couldn't.

At night she raved on and on. Martha tried to get her to quiet down and go to sleep, but neither one was getting much sleep. Martha was near the breaking point herself. Everyone was upset that she had taken Josephine out of the nursing home.

Martha heard her speak at night, "Lois is going to come get me and take me to her house. I'm just waiting for Lois. She's my best sister."

Other times she would say, "Don't make me leave this room." She was more aware of what was going on than people thought. She never forgot the nursing home experience. She would reason to herself, "Martha's the bad one. Let's see. I have two daughters. Sometimes I think there's another one. She calls me Mama. Helen, no it's not Helen. She lives far away and she's the frail one. It must be Martha."

Sometimes she would tell herself, "Don't cry." Martha had rarely if ever seen Josephine cry. It was heartbreaking. Martha did a lot of crying herself, like every morning in the bathroom after she had showered and dressed Josephine and sat her down for breakfast. And again at night she would pray, "God, just let her die in her sleep." She knew that her life would not have meaning without her mother. She never felt alone going anywhere with her. She also knew she would miss her mother when she was gone, but she would not want her back like this. She was not like she used to be.

Years later, Martha thought that if she had made a tape recording telling her mother that she was back home and would stay there, and go to daycare like before, and keep playing it over and over, then her mother would be reassured and become content again. But she did not think of it, and eventually the Alzheimer's would have taken over anyway.

At daycare Josephine rambled on all day like she did at home. They began to sit her facing the television set away from the others to drown out her mutterings. When Martha asked them if she was disturbing them, they said no, it didn't bother them; they were okay with her.

One day, Josephine had finished lunch and walked from the dining room to the recreation room with a fork in her hand. "Ms. Josie, what are you doing taking that fork with you?"

"I'm going to stab Martha with it."

They told Martha who said she wasn't afraid. But after thinking about it, she often locked her bedroom door. At times Josephine didn't recognize Martha. Martha would put her on the commode and when she went back to help her out, Josephine didn't want her near. Martha made a name tag with *Martha* on it, put it around her neck on a string, and then Josephine would allow her to help her.

Helen came to visit again and could see some change in Josephine. She tried to help Josephine and do things for her, but she shook her off and said, "No, I want Martha." And sometimes she refused Martha's help, too.

This frightened Helen. Josephine had never yelled or shoved like that before. When Helen saw Martha put on the name tag and then Josephine let Martha help her, Helen really got upset. When she got Martha alone, she said, "I'm going to help you put her in another nursing home and you have to leave her there."

The doctor said the same when Martha went back to get him to authorize admittance. He said, "Do not take her out this time."

The girls found a smaller nursing home which would accept her. They thought that it being smaller, she would get better care. They got a room down at the end of the hall where it would be quiet, and put some of her furniture in it. It was a private room and the girls paid the difference in cost. When they talked to the admissions person, they asked that she be put in a wheelchair only to go distances, and that she be encouraged to use her walker so she could get some exercise and flexing. They promised this, but of course they didn't, they just left her sitting in her wheelchair.

Martha insisted that Helen bolster her in admitting their mom. She felt bad about doing it again, and needed support, so they asked Bonnie, Helen's step-daughter, who had always visited Josephine, to go with them to move her in and she did. The girls had told Josephine that they had found her an "apartment" and that she would have people to help her, with nurses around, and a dining room with meals. Josephine knew she did not remember things and got confused, and she was angry, but unable to do anything herself and accepted it.

Martha took pictures of Josephine in her new room, and later when the pictures were developed, she saw that her mother was swollen head to toe, her face, body, everything. She had extensive fluid retention and must have already been developing congestive heart failure. She had no evidence of it in either of her exams for nursing home admittance or with her regular doctor, and Martha wondered how she could have just thought Josephine had gained weight and not noticed the swelling.

Helen and Martha visited with Josephine and walked her around the home and to the dining room for lunch. Helen sent Martha to the ice cream parlor in the same block for ice cream, and they ate it together with Josephine in the courtyard. They were very optimistic that things would be better for Josephine there.

Helen went back to her home now that her mother was settled in, and called Martha every day. Sometimes Martha called Helen and Lois from the nursing home so Josephine could talk to them. Josephine wanted Lois to know where she was and still believed and hoped that Lois would come get her. Lois was older now, as well, and unable to take on that responsibility.

The staff was short; in fact, one aide sometimes had sixteen patients to care for who in worse shape than Josephine. Again, if water was put in the room, no one poured her a glass or saw that she drank it, and water was not always put in her room. Josephine was wheeled to the dining room for meals, and to bingo games and activities. Otherwise, she was left to sit in the wheelchair with no exercise. At first, Martha tried not to be there all the time, to give her a chance to get adjusted, but she did go every day. She didn't know the extent of the neglect yet. Again, they were ordering tests and giving her medicines for conditions she never had before, and Martha did not learn this for a while.

A beautician volunteered to do the ladies' hair once a week, but the first week, Martha realized Josephine's hair had not been done. When she asked the nurses, she was given a vague answer. Bathing was to be done in a tank of sorts. To Martha's knowledge, it was never used on anyone, only promised. One aide had many clients and did the best she could, but couldn't keep up. When the ombudsmen program was called, they said there was no guideline on how many clients per aide.

Martha asked if she could use the shampoo sink to wash Josephine's hair, because it had been over two weeks and she had never gotten a shampoo. She was allowed to do so. Martha was spending much more time caring for her mother now than ever, plus the daily drive. She had gotten better care at home. Bonnie went to see her as often as she could and she always brought something. Once it was a jar of candy with Maw Maw Josephine written on it.

Martha paid Molly to visit and sit with Josephine. She requested that Molly ask Josephine how she liked it, and to feel out her attitude about where she was. Molly did not ask that. She took the friend position personally, and either did not want to upset Josephine or to implicate herself as being a party to her confinement, which of course, she wasn't.

Martha often challenged the admissions person and the director about conditions. They pretended everything was fine. Martha always tried to find something to praise in order to motivate them to treat Josephine well. One day she walked in to find Josephine still in bed at eleven, and wet. When she went to find an aide they did come and clean her. Again, if a client was not ready to get up and get dressed, they left them alone. There was an older black aide who was very good and efficient. She knew how to coax the client to agree to what she needed to do. Josephine liked her, but usually she was assigned to the other section. There was a young white aide who really did her best, but often could not get to everyone.

Many of the clients were incontinent, and supplies were short. There were no baby wipes or such and they used towels to clean up excrement and threw them away, so linens were scarce. Martha brought some from home and wrote Josie on them. She used them herself to wash her mom and took them home to launder. Martha was charged for two cases of adult diapers for Josephine, when Martha knew Josephine didn't need that many, even if she had been changed regularly, which she wasn't. She suspected they were used on others who could not afford them.

The laundry room did an efficient job, and the kitchen did also. Recreation was not lacking, either. There were aides or nurses who fed those who couldn't help themselves, but they were outnumbered and time ran out, especially since those who could feed themselves well were served first. Martha made sure she was there for breakfast and lunch to see that Josephine ate and drank. Sometimes Josephine had to be prompted to pick up her fork, but she could eat and swallow. Martha tried to avoid being there for bedtime because she knew Josephine did not want to stay there at night, and thought if she wasn't there it would be easier to get her to bed. Or maybe she felt less guilty going to the home they had shared if she didn't have to tell her mom, "Goodnight, I'm going home to the house you used to live in." Then she found out that Josephine would dawdle in the dining room to avoid bed, or ask for a sandwich later, which they gave her.

Josephine had been in this second nursing home less than two weeks when Martha arrived at 11 AM and found Josephine lying on the floor in her room. When Martha called her name, she opened her eyes, but she was disoriented, and wasn't aware that she was on the floor. She had been lying there so long that there were dried urine stains on her red warm-up pants.

Martha went to the nurse's station to get help. She railed about how no one had noticed that she was on the floor, and how long had she been lying there, all night? Perhaps she had injured her head or something else. So they got her up and called the ambulance to send her to the hospital. Martha went with her mother. All her vital signs were checked; she was X-Rayed then admitted to the hospital and placed on the cardiology floor. She had a blood clot in her leg and the leg was very swollen, so she was given a blood thinner, along with other medicines.

Dr. Stevenson was the best cardiologist in the hospital and a very caring man. He talked to Martha at length. Martha poured out her struggles to care for her mother, and all her medical history and told him that prior to being in a nursing home, all she had wrong was

Alzheimer's and arthritis, and had never had heart trouble.

Whenever Dr. Stevenson entered the room, Martha joked and said, "Look, Mom, it's your good looking doctor." The doctor kept Martha informed on all his findings and everything he did and prescribed. He gently and carefully tried to warn her that her mother would not live out the year, and if she had to choose between treatments and comfort for her mother, she should lean toward comfort. Martha knew the resiliency of her mother and knew her ability to recover under the right conditions and didn't believe she would die.

Dr. Stevenson told Martha many times that he had never seen anyone so adamant about caring for their mother. He and others tried to make Martha a hero for all she had done for her mother, but she couldn't accept that. She knew that she had failed. She knew the despair of her mother, and the horror of her fear of nursing homes, yet she had placed her in two of them. She cried and prayed about it over and over, even after this scripture came to her, "The Lord led you into the wilderness, to humble you, and to know what is in your heart." But she didn't like what she saw in her heart and found little consolation in all the praise of others. Later she felt that God was saying, "No matter how many chances you would have take care of your mother, you would still not do it perfectly. You were in an impossible situation. It's in the past, accept that."

Dr. Stevenson kept Josephine in the hospital several days for tests, and tried to get the blood clot and heart condition under control.

Martha continually told her mother she was in the hospital. Josephine could cope with being in the hospital, not the nursing home. She was very aware of what was happening, and it was like she did not even have Alzheimer's.

Upon hearing that her mother was in the hospital, Helen came again to be with them. Helen took the night shift, Martha the day shift staying with Josephine. Her leg was still swollen and painful, and her breathing was getting more labored, but she knew both her daughters and loved them. When her daughters explained what the nurses would do, Josephine did not resist or complain. She still had an appetite and ate most of her food with their help. She had developed dead tissue on her heels in the nursing home from lack of circulation, so Martha got her some bed boots to try to prevent contact with the bed. Nurses cleaned and scraped dead tissue off. This was very painful, also.

David Dickey, the head deacon of Family Worship Center, visited Josephine in the hospital and prayed, and a few days later, Rev. Dave Smith also visited and prayed. Martha knew them well, and was grateful for their prayers.

After a few days the doctor released Josephine back into the nursing home. Martha and Helen had spent most of that day with her there, but went home to eat. Helen was tired from spending nights in the hospital and asked Bonnie to visit Josephine after work and give a progress report.

Bonnie called to report that no one had cleaned her wounds, but since she called it to their attention, they did. Josephine, however, was not too happy about having them handle her, causing her more pain.

The next day, Helen and Martha got a call from the nursing home telling them that they had sent her back to the hospital, so they went there. Dr. Stevenson said that her condition had worsened, and her heart and lungs were under duress. Martha took Helen home to rest because she was to spend the night with Josephine.

Josephine had developed a bad yeast infection from all the antibiotics and all the sugar laden food in the nursing home and hospital. The doctor prescribed a fungal pill which was so powerful that only one was given. Martha said, "Doctor, she's overrun with yeast and if she gets a pill this strong without going on a sugar free diet a few days her body will be overwhelmed with yeast die-off." He said that would not happen, so Josephine took the pill.

The next day, Josephine's respiratory system was full of fluid. Martha tried to entice Josephine to eat, but she did not want food and just drank juice. In the afternoon, Martha asked an aide to help bathe her and put a clean gown on Josephine. She had the same gown since being admitted again and it had dried blood on it. Hospitals also were not able to get around to bathing all the patients regularly. Josephine was more comfortable after the bath and clean bed and gown, and was drifting off to sleep. Martha placed her chair where Josephine could see her when she opened her eyes. She said, "Mom, I'm going to be sitting right here reading the paper if you need me, and I'm going to go get Helen at five o'clock to come stay with you tonight."

Josephine said, "I love y'all."

"We love you too, Mama."

In about an hour, Josephine said, "Martha, take my watch and hold it."

Martha started getting a funny feeling that something was going on, because it was similar to when

Richard was going to the operating room and Josephine held his watch. It was like Josephine knew she was going somewhere. She took the watch and put it on her own wrist, and pulled her chair up to the bed. She held her Mom's hand and watched her carefully.

"I love you and Helen."

"We love you, too, Mama. Helen's going to come spend the night with you." Martha was supposed to get Helen in an hour to take her shift, but Martha did not want to leave her mother's side or to phone Helen where Josephine could hear her. She did not want her mom to pass away alone. She did say, "Mom, you know what Jill and Garry did to you; God's Word says you have to forgive others whether they deserve it or not for Him to be able to forgive you, and we've all made mistakes. You need to forgive Jill and Garry."

Josephine, with the last of her strength said, "...forgive Jill and Garry."

Martha kissed her mother and held her hand and prayed, asking God to send his angels for her. It was just minutes until the breaths got less frequent, with more time elapsing between them. Then there were no more, and the last one was expelled.

Martha called Helen and told her Josephine had died, why she had not wanted to leave to pick her up, and asked if she wanted to come now. She said no, there wasn't any use now. Martha waited fifteen minutes before going out into the hall to ask for Dr. Stevenson. Josephine had a living will, and after all the pain and torment of her last month or so, she was ready to go. Martha suspected that Josephine knew she was going when she asked her to take her watch.

When she did go out of the room to tell the staff, they spoke of resuscitation. Martha said, "Do not do anything until you talk to Dr. Stevenson. My mother has a living will saying no resuscitation and it's in the car if I have to get it."

They called the doctor and he came immediately. He asked if Martha wanted an autopsy, she said, "No, no use in that. It's over." He arranged for the funeral home to take the body, and Martha also called them and made an appointment for Helen and her to see them the next day to make arrangements.

It was about six PM on Wednesday, and Monday was Memorial Day. Six more days was too long so they planned on a Friday burial. This was not much notice for folks to come to a wake and a funeral.

The obituary ran in Baton Rouge and not in the town of Josephine's long time residence, Plaquemine. Many of those who knew her did not know she had died, even though she was going to be buried beside Richard. Martha called Mrs. Futrell and asked her to tell some of the people they knew.

Martha called a pastor, Reverend Loren Larson, from Family Worship Center to see if he could officiate in the funeral. He said he was glad to. Martha would get the information that he would need to him soon, and asked him if he could get the song, *It Matters To Him About You,* and play it during the ceremony. He said, "I can sing it."

"Of course, I wasn't thinking. Thank you. That's the song Mom and I listened to over and over in the last two years. I played it just before she went to sleep"

Martha told him she would write a Eulogy for him, thinking Reverend Larson would read it, but he said, "You will give the Eulogy."

"Oh, okay. Well, thank you and I'll talk to you tomorrow."

Rev. Larson has been with the Jimmy Swaggart Ministry many years and served as FWC Choir and Music Director, and head of FWC Prison Ministry as well as being a professor and President of World Evangelism Bible College and Seminary.

Martha typed a list of names that Reverend Larson would need like the names of Josephine's deceased husband, parents, and brother, and her surviving sisters, brother, and daughters, and how to pronounce them. He was from the northwest and was not accustomed to Cajun names. She was trying to think of everything they would need beforehand.

"Martha, stop that and go to bed," Helen said, always thinking of her sister's well-being.

"I can't. I have to get this done tonight. There isn't much time, and we're going to have to go to the funeral home in Plaquemine in the morning."

Martha thought back to when she was in Tennessee longing to be near her mother and thinking she may have ten more years to live. The date that her divorce was final and she could go to Louisiana was May 23, and it was ten years ago to the day her mother died! That gave her consolation that God had been in all of this.

The next morning, they worked out the arrangements with the funeral home, finding a nice casket, but the cost of the funeral was so much more than they expected. Josephine had already purchased a crypt with Richard, so they didn't have that expense, just the stone covering and inscription. But there were standard charges for things that Martha had already taken care of, and they would not adjust the price.

Helen and Martha picked out clothing for Josephine and a nice scarf to place in her hands, rather than the rosary that Catholics used. Martha had long since disclaimed being Catholic and told the aunts and cousins they would not be reciting the rosary. They brought her favorite necklace for her neck, and also brought her favorite green sweater, a slip and other undies. They did not bother with stockings and a skirt, but the director was very upset with them and said it didn't matter if only the waist up was visible; she had to be fully clothed. Everything was done with total dignity. Chastised, they went to the store and got a nice skirt that matched the sweater, and stockings.

They told the lady who did the makeup and hair that Josephine wanted to look real nice, and to roll her hair and put lifelike makeup. They finally had to give her a lipstick so it would be red enough. It just wasn't Josephine without the red lipstick. The lady did a fabulous job and the result was gorgeous.

The sisters crossed the street to go to the local florist and chose a really beautiful floral arrangement for the casket. The florist did a great job on the flowers. Family Worship Center sent a lovely arrangement, as well as Bonnie and all Helen's step children. Letty also sent a beautiful basket of fragrant white roses. She was a constant friend and encourager. Helen's friend in Texas also sent a massive vase of colorful flowers.

Some of the family and friends were only able to attend either the wake or the funeral, not both, because of distance, so there were not many people. The pastor and his wife of the little church they had attended in Port Allen where Martha had her trailer came to the wake. Josephine had liked their church because it reminded her of when Bitsy took her to church as a child. He and his wife gave their condolences and the pastor said he would be happy to do the service if needed. Martha was overcome and said how grateful she was that he would offer, but she had asked Reverend Larson, a pastor from the church in Baton Rouge where she now attended.

Standing in front of the funeral home, Martha watched for Reverend Larson to arrive on Friday, the day of the burial. He was not familiar with Plaquemine, but arrived on time. Martha gave him the list she had prepared the night before and he spoke to the funeral director to coordinate events. He began the service with the song; *It Matters To Him About You.* He had a beautiful deep singing voice. Then using the background Martha had given him, he spoke to the family and friends. His sermon was about King David in the Bible who had sinned with Bathsheba. When discovered, he repented and acknowledged his sin; he wept, fasted, and prayed, but still the baby died. Then he rose up, washed himself, praised God and ate. His servants were amazed. But he said, "Now he is dead, why should I fast? Can I bring him back? I shall go to him but he shall not return to me."

Reverend Larson's message was that we should not prolong mourning, because if we are right with the Lord in trusting what Jesus did for us on the cross, as born again children of God we shall see our loved ones again in Heaven.

When Martha gave the Eulogy, this is what she said: "First, I want to thank all the friends and family for their support. Many times it seems we are alone, and then you see the people who were with you.

"Mom was a remarkable woman who was first a wife and devoted mother. Her talents were too numerous to name them all, the best cook, an amazing seamstress, she spent quality time with her daughters, teaching them valuable lessons: reading, homemaking, gardening, fishing, pecan and berry picking and economics. She worked hard alongside her husband on the farm, planting, tilling, harvesting, canning, and raising livestock. Her pleasures were simple. Many said she had a hard life.

"She remained in good health all her life until the end and never complained or acknowledged the pain of her final days."

Martha looked at her mother in the casket and continued, "She looks real sophisticated now. She used to always wear a kerchief on her head so she would not be cold. Once I teased her, asking if she wanted to be buried in her kerchief. She said no, I want to look good. I won't be cold then." (Everyone who knew her and her kerchief laughed at that.)

Martha continued, "She was raised Catholic, but enjoyed Pentecostal Church, saying it reminded her of her visits as a girl to a Baptist Church where a black woman took her. In the Pentecostal churches she always said the prayer of salvation along with the preacher out loud and meant it. As a Catholic she knew Jesus as her Savior, but as a Pentecostal she knew Jesus wanted to be Lord over her life. I thank God that Helen and I could spend so much time with Mom. And Mom--we've already said our goodbyes, but we'll soon see you in Glory, where love is so much deeper than even a mother's love on earth."

With not many young men in the family, three employees of the funeral home volunteered to be pallbearers. One of them was the director. When the funeral was over and Helen and Martha thanked him and the others for being pallbearers, he said, "After attending the service, I am honored to be her pallbearer and serve Josephine in any way I could."

Josephine was buried next to Richard in Grace Memorial Park on a pleasant day in May. Everyone said they had never seen a more beautiful funeral. Just as in the hour of her death, her funeral service and burial seemed almost ...*holy*.

www.ingramcontent.com/pod-product-compliance
Lightning Source LLC
Chambersburg PA
CBHW031233090426
42742CB00007B/180